EDUCATION, DISABILITY AND SOCIAL POLICY

Edited by Steve Haines and David Ruebain

First published in Great Britain in 2011 by

The Policy Press
University of Bristol
Fourth Floor
Beacon House
Queen's Road
Bristol BS8 1QU
UK

Tel +44 (0)117 331 4054
Fax +44 (0)117 331 4093
e-mail tpp-info@bristol.ac.uk
www.policypress.co.uk

North American office:
The Policy Press
c/o International Specialized Books Services (ISBS)
920 NE 58th Avenue, Suite 300
Portland, OR 97213-3786, USA
Tel +1 503 287 3093
Fax +1 503 280 8832
e-mail info@isbs.com

© The Policy Press 2011

British Library Cataloguing in Publication Data
A catalogue record for this book is available from the British Library.

Library of Congress Cataloging-in-Publication Data
A catalog record for this book has been requested.

ISBN 978 1 84742 336 8 paperback
ISBN 978 1 84742 337 5 hardcover

The right of Steve Haines and David Ruebain to be identified as editors of this work has been asserted by them in accordance with the 1988 Copyright, Designs and Patents Act.

Cover design by Janna Broadfoot.
Front cover: image kindly supplied by www.istock.com
Printed and bound in Great Britain by Hobbs, Southampton
The Policy Press uses environmentally responsible print partners.

Contents

Acknowledgements

As editors we have been fortunate to have benefited from the support of a number of friends; chief among them Len Barton and Patrick Diamond, to whom we owe a huge debt of gratitude for their advice and comments on early drafts. Conversations with Tom Shakespeare, Gerrard Quinn, Emily Saltz, Geoff Whitty and Paul Steven Miller (who tragically died in October 2010) shaped our early thinking. Kate Haines encouraged an idea to become a proposal, and a proposal a book, and gave endless love and support every step of the way. At The Policy Press, Karen Bowler, Leila Ebrahimi and Kathryn King have been a constant support, offering enthusiasm for the project balanced with timely constructive criticism.

Author biographies

Cherie Booth is a leading barrister specialising in employment, public, international and human rights law. She became a Queen's Counsel in 1995 and set up, with 21 other prominent barristers, Matrix Chambers, which has built a reputation in human rights and public law. A strong campaigner on women's and children's issues, Cherie has set up the Cherie Blair Foundation for Women. She is also a Patron of the disability charity Scope.

Anne Borsay is Professor of Healthcare and Medical Humanities in the College of Human and Health Sciences at Swansea University. Her principal research interest is the social and cultural history of disability, and she is committed to teasing out the implications of perspectives from history, literature and the visual arts for contemporary policy and practice. Her single-authored publications include *Disabled People in the Community: A Study of Housing, Health and Welfare Services* (Bedford Square Press, 1986), *Medicine and Charity in Georgian Bath: A Social History of the General Infirmary, c.1739–1830* (Ashgate, 1999) and *Disability and Social Policy in Britain since 1750: A History of Exclusion* (Palgrave Macmillan, 2005). She is currently writing a cultural history of disability in Britain for Palgrave Macmillan and co-editing, with Dr Pamela Dale of Exeter University, a collection of essays entitled *Disabled Children: Contested Caring, c.1850–1979*. Anne sits on the editorial board of *Disability and Society* and is a member of the Wellcome Trust's Medical History and Humanities Funding Committee.

Marc Bush is Head of Research and Public Policy at the disability charity Scope. He has an academic and research background in sociological research and a long-standing interest in disability issues, in particular, constructions of challenging social behaviour, mental issues, adolescence and human value. Marc has advised organisations on approaches to social change, social action and prospective policy analysis and contributed to parliamentary, governmental and non-departmental public body reviews into services for disabled children as they transition from children to adult services. He has led a number of policy-influencing research projects that focus on disabled children's human rights and the position of families with disabled children in modern society. Marc is also the trustee of a small, children's rights organisation in England.

Rory Cobb is a teacher of children with visual impairment and has worked in a number of roles for the Royal National Institute of Blind People (RNIB) since the 1980s. He has a special interest in access to the curriculum and examinations, working closely with awarding bodies and government agencies to improve provision for blind and partially sighted learners in public exams. Rory also coordinates RNIB's support for education professionals and is the lead tutor on Partners in Learning, RNIB's accredited course for teaching assistants. He is a member of the executive committee of Visual Impairment: Education and Welfare (VIEW), the professional association of teachers of the visually impaired, and has been chair of the annual VIEW conference since 2003.

Neil Crowther is Human Rights Programme Director at the Equality and Human Rights Commission. He previously held the post of Disability Programme Director. He has written widely on the potential of the capabilities approach to transform the approach of public policy and services to disabled people, including in relation to employment and social care. Before joining the Equality and Human Rights Commission, he was Head of Policy at the Disability Rights Commission where he led the development of its 'Disability Agenda', a forward-facing public policy agenda designed to advance disability rights over the 2000s. He started his career at the Royal National Institute of Blind People.

Steve Haines was formerly Head of Policy at the Disability Rights Commission and Head of Policy and Strategy for Save the Children's UK Programme. He has provided advice regarding young disabled people in education to the Nuffield Review of 14–19 Education, the Learning and Skills Council and QCA's Curriculum Futures. He now works in the Prime Minister's Office in Rwanda.

Ann Lewis is Emeritus Professor at the University of Birmingham (UK) where she was until recently research leader for a unique, 35-strong, academic group focusing on children with special needs or disabilities. She is also Honorary Professor at the University of Warwick (UK). She has a long-standing interest in the 'voice' of disabled children, in particular, conceptual and methodological aspects of realising such 'voice' authentically in diverse contexts. This is reflected in her research (e.g. 'The experiences of disabled pupils and their families' [2004–07] funded by the Disability Rights Commission), publications (including *Researching Children's Perspectives* [Open University Press, 2000], edited with Professor Geoff Lindsay) and various research consultancies, as well as her role as an Advisory Group member for BBC Children in Need. She is engaged at national and international levels with research and critiques of policy concerning provision for children with special needs or disabilities. She was a member of the Advisory Group for the Lamb Inquiry (2008–10), set up by the UK government to examine ways of increasing parental confidence in the special educational needs (SEN) assessment process. Related to this, she was specialist advisor to the preceding House of Commons Select Committees on SEN (2006, 2007). A key aspect of her work concerns the extent to which children with special needs or disabilities require demonstrably different teaching strategies from those used with other children (e.g. see *Special Teaching for Special Children: Pedagogies for Inclusion?* [Open University Press, 2005], edited with Professor Brahm Norwich).

Olga Miller is a Senior Lecturer at the Institute of Education, University of London. Dr Miller also has a national role in teacher education with the Royal National Institute of Blind People (RNIB). Dr Miller is a researcher and qualified teacher whose main area of specialism is disabilities of sight in childhood. Her key remit is training teachers to work with children and young people who have little or no sight. She was formerly Head of the RNIB Children's Policy Unit and currently is a member of the RNIB Evidence and Impact Team.

Sheila Riddell is Director of the Centre for Research in Education, Inclusion and Diversity (CREID) at the University of Edinburgh. She is the author of *Policy and Practice in Special Educational Needs: Additional Support for Learning* (Dunedin Academic Press, 2006) and co-author of *Improving Disabled Students' Learning in Higher Education* (RoutledgeFalmer, 2009), *Disabled Students in Higher Education: Perspectives on Widening Access and Changing Policy* (RoutledgeFalmer, 2005) and *The Learning Society and People with Learning Difficulties* (The Policy Press, 2001).

David Ruebain is Chief Executive of the Equality Challenge Unit, the equality organisation for the UK higher education sector. He was formerly Director of Legal Policy at the Equality and Human Rights Commission and former Head of Education and Disability Law at Levenes Solicitors. David is the winner of RADAR's People of the Year Award for Achievement in the Furtherance of Human Rights of Disabled People in the UK, was so shortlisted for the Law Society's Gazette Centenary Award for Lifetime Achievement – Human Rights, and was listed as one of 25 Most Influential Disabled People in the UK by *Disability Now* magazine.

Philippa Russell is the Chair of the Prime Minister's Standing Commission on Carers, launched by Prime Minister Gordon Brown in 2007. She was Disability Policy Adviser to the National Children's Bureau and formerly a Commissioner with the Disability Rights Commission and Director of the Council for Disabled Children. She is an Honorary Fellow of the Royal College of Paediatrics and Child Health and a Fellow of the Royal Society of Arts. She has Honorary Doctorates from the University of York and King Alfred's College of Higher Education, Winchester, for her work with disabled children and their families and is an Honorary Fellow of the University of Central Lancashire. She was awarded an OBE for her work with children with special educational needs and their families; a CBE for services to disabled people; and a DBE in 2009 for services to disabled people and family carers. In 1990, she was awarded the Rose Fitzgerald Kennedy Centenary International Award for women who have contributed to the field of learning disability. She was also awarded the 4Children Lifetime Achievement Award in 2004 for her work in developing childcare and other services for disabled children and their families. In 2005, she was awarded the Royal Association of Disability and Rehabilitation (RADAR) Lifetime Achievement Award for the furtherance of the human and civil rights of disabled people. She is the parent of a son with a learning disability and has wide contacts with voluntary and user organisations with an interest in disabled children, young people and their families. In this context, she is a trustee of the National Family Carers Network and the National Development Team for Inclusion and is Chair of MOVE (a new charity established under the auspices of the Prince of Wales' National Disability Partnership to support the inclusion of children and adults with complex disabilities in school and community).

Ruth Scott is Director of Policy and Campaigns at the disability charity Scope. She has worked in the disability sector for over a decade, leading policy and legislative work on a range of areas including education, civil and human rights, employment, and inclusive democracy. Ruth has a particular interest in social change including the development and implementation of theories of change, rights frameworks and attitudinal and behaviour change. She was heavily involved in the disability sector's work on influencing the approach of government to the incorporation of the UN Convention on the Rights of Persons with

Disabilities (CRPD) and non-regression of rights in the formulation of the 2010 Equality Act. She is currently the Chair of the policy group of the Disability Charities Consortium (DCC), an informal network of seven of the largest disability charities in the UK. Ruth is also a trustee of a small development charity that supports infrastructure and capacity-building projects in Malawi.

Paul Simpson is the Executive Officer of the British Association of Teachers of the Deaf (BATOD), the professional association of Teachers of the Deaf. He qualified as a Teacher of the Deaf in 1986 and has worked in a secondary school for deaf children where he was housemaster, a peripatetic teacher, a head of specialist support services and a head of a primary school for deaf children. He also works as a teaching practice supervisor for teachers training as Teachers of the Deaf and has worked for the Royal National Institute of Deaf People (RNID) on some educational publications. He is involved in Europe through his role as the President of the Fédération Européenne d'Associations de Professeurs de Déficients Auditifs (FEAPDA [the European Federation of Associations of Teachers of the Deaf]).

Liz Todd is Professor of Educational Inclusion at the University of Newcastle, having had roles as a teacher, educational psychologist and lecturer at the University of the South Pacific. Her research interests are in finding out how professionals can help without getting in the way of the knowledges and resources of their punters, and this includes looking at extended schools, pupil voice and narrative practices. Her 2007 book, *Partnerships for Inclusive Education* (Routledge), was shortlisted for the NASEN/TES (National Association for Special Educational Needs/Times Education Supplement) inclusive education prize and she has published a book (*Beyond the School Gates: Can Full Service and Extended Schools Overcome Disadvantage?* [Routledge, 2011]) with Alan Dyson and Colleen Cummings on whether extended schools can beat disadvantage.

Nigel Utton is a primary school head teacher and passionate campaigner for inclusive education. He is a trustee of the Alliance for Inclusive Education and Chair of Heading for Inclusion – an organisation for educational professionals dedicated to the principles and practice of inclusion. As a white Englishman, with black African and Ashkenazi Jewish heritage, inclusion is built into his very DNA.

After studying Russian, French and psycholinguistics at the University of East Anglia, Nigel did a variety of jobs ranging from tax officer to toy librarian before finally realising he was destined to be a primary school teacher in 1991. He became a teacher of Re-evaluation Counselling in 1992 and has used these skills to work effectively with children with 'behavioural difficulties'. He has written articles on inclusion, organised international workshops on educational change and led workshops and given talks on inclusion and ending racism, sexism and homophobia. His main goal currently is to show that inclusion works with real children in a real school! In March 2011 Nigel's school was judged 'outstanding' for its social, moral, cultural and spiritual aspects of learning.

Elisabet Weedon is Deputy Director of the Centre for Research in Education Inclusion and Diversity (CREID) at the University of Edinburgh. Her main research interests are in the area of lifelong learning and social justice. She has been involved in research into the experiences of disabled students in higher education, the use of restorative practices in education and dispute resolution in the area of additional support needs. Current projects include an investigation of the experiences and outcomes for Muslim pupils, research into lifelong learning in Europe, and learning in the workplace.

Preface

This book is a major contribution to the debate about education, social policy and disability in the UK. It is a powerful reminder that we need to think far more expansively about the future of policy and provision as it impacts on children with disabilities and special educational needs (SEN). The Green Paper published by the Coalition government aims to show how government can respond to the diverse needs of pupils and parents, ensuring access to an educational setting of choice – whether it is a mainstream school, academy or special school.

The strong emphasis on empowerment and choice will be welcomed in many quarters. But it also raises significant dilemmas, most notably how to prevent a system of free choice from aggravating historically ingrained inequalities of outcome and opportunity for children with disabilities and SEN. This book lays bare such tensions and explores how policy can advance the cause of all children as the cornerstone of a fairer, more equal society.

Patrick Diamond, Senior Research Fellow, Policy Network
and Former Group Director for Strategy at the Equality and
Human Rights Commission,
October 2010

This book raises several fundamentally important issues and questions, not only in relation to disability, but also, importantly, in relation to the conceptual and practical concerns over inclusive values, ideas and practices. It is essential reading for all those who are concerned with the pursuit of effective change, which raises questions about the nature and purpose of education and the removal of all barriers to participation for all learners.

Given the global and national economic and political context, the question of disability needs to be understood in a broader context of inequalities, exclusions and discrimination. Thus, the struggle for a political economy of disability, in which the question and demands of human rights, social justice and entitlements under law have become increasingly urgent and necessary.

One of the disturbing aspects of the contemporary position with regard to policy and its implementation is the extent of the differences that are increasingly obvious between commendable rhetoric and actual reality. The extent of the struggle required for effective change to be established and maintained leaves no room for complacency.

Len Barton, Executive Director of IDRIS,
Emeritus Professor of Inclusive Education, University of London
October 2010

Foreword

Please do not see this as a book that is just for the specialists – activists in the field of disability education talking to activists in the field of disability education – but as a book for anyone who cares about young people and about putting into practice the values of the Universal Declaration of Human Rights of 1948 and later instruments such as the 1989 Convention on the Rights of the Child and the 2006 Convention on the Rights of Persons with Disabilities (ratified by the United Kingdom in 2009).

Article 1 of the Universal Declaration famously declares that 'All human beings are born free and equal in dignity and rights'. But in a factual sense we all know that this is not true. We all come into this world differently endowed. Some of our endowment is external – riches, loving parents, congenial surroundings; some of it is internal – our physical and mental capacities and personalities. What we eventually become is shaped by the complex interaction of these internal and external forces together with what happens next.

So what should happen next? If all human beings are to be free and equal in dignity and rights, they have to be given the means to become functioning members of the grown-up world. Everyone, says Article 26(1) of the Universal Declaration, has the right to education. Education, says Article 26(2), shall be directed to the full development of the human personality and to the strengthening of respect of human rights and fundamental freedoms. The only halfway positive right in the European Declaration of Human Rights of 1950 is in the First Protocol: 'No one shall be denied the right to education'. Though narrowly construed as a right of 'access to such educational facilities as the state provides for such pupils' (as Lord Bingham put it in *A v Head teacher and Governors of Lord Grey School* [2006] UKHL 14, [2006] 2 AC 363, para 24), in this country we have decided that we have a duty to educate everyone. As the Warnock Committee put it in 1978:

> education, as we conceive it, is a good, and a specifically human good, to which all human beings are entitled. There exists, therefore, a clear obligation to educate the most severely disabled for no other reason than that they are human. No civilised society can be content just to look after these children: it must all the time seek ways of helping them, however slowly, towards the educational goals we have identified. (*Special Educational Needs: Report of the Committee*

of Enquiry into the Education of Handicapped Children and Young People, Cmnd 7212, London: HMSO, Section 1.7)

The question, then, is not *whether* this is to be done. The majority of the Supreme Court (in *A v Essex County Council* [2010] UKSC 33) thought that providing little or no education for a severely disabled child for more than 18 months at least raised an issue of whether his rights under the First Protocol had been violated.

The question is *how* it is to be done. Disabilities are many and various. Some are creatures of law, having nothing to do with the actual capacities of the individual human being. Until the 1919 Sex Disqualification (Removal) Act, being female was a disability in the United Kingdom. Until the decision of the Supreme Court in *Brown v Board of Education* (347 US 483) in 1954, being black was a disability in the United States. The solution found in both cases was to behave as if the disability did not exist and treat women as men and black as white. It is easy to see these as artificial barriers, readily ignored. But even that is controversial. Do girls learn differently from boys, and vice versa, and do both, therefore, need different forms of teaching in order to reach their full potential?

So how much more complicated is the question when it is quite clear that some differences do need some different forms of teaching. We can all agree that people who cannot see should have access to the written word in other ways, that people who cannot hear should have access to the spoken word in other ways, and that people who have difficulty moving should have access to the places where otherwise they cannot go. We can all agree that none of these should be barriers to achieving an individual's full potential. Gone, we hope, are the days when a blind or deaf person or a wheelchair user could not aspire to become, for example, a High Court judge. But we can still debate about what are the best ways to enable that potential to be fulfilled and even more about who are the best people to make the decision.

I fear that the barriers are much more difficult to surmount when they are mental or psychological rather than physical. How do we know what a person's full potential may be? But mentally or psychologically disabled students have undoubtedly benefited from the determined stance taken by and on behalf of physically disabled students, just as mentally and psychologically disabled adults have benefited from the determined stance taken by and on behalf of physically disabled adults.

The clear message to emerge from the various contributions to this book is that one size does not fit all. Integration or separation are not goals in themselves, but means towards what ought to be the same goal for all. This has not changed since the Universal Declaration in 1948. As Article 24(1) of the UN Convention on the Rights of Persons with Disabilities now puts it:

> States Parties shall ensure an inclusive education system at all levels and life long learning directed to ... the full development of human potential and sense of dignity and self worth and the strengthening of respect for human rights, fundamental freedoms and human diversity.

So we should all read this book for an exploration of how these fundamental values can best be put into practice in the thoughtful and mature society that we all hope ours to be.

Lady Hale
Justice of the Supreme Court of the United Kingdom
30 September 2010

Introduction

David Ruebain and Steve Haines

This book considers the progress that has been made since the 1980s in educational provision in the UK for disabled students, including children and young people in schools and adults in higher education. The authors, drawn from a range of pedagogic, professional and activist backgrounds, consider the advances, challenges and difficulties that make up the current experience of disabled students and look to the future of what might come next in the pursuit of greater educational opportunities.

As editors, our own starting point is to consider these issues through the perspective of the social model of disability; a model theorists and activists have long advocated, albeit in various guises. In short, this juxtaposes a disabled person's impairment with the response that society has to it, so that rather than perceiving disabled people as subject to overarching deficiencies caused by their impairment, instead it is the environment and arrangements through which disabled people live that often cause the barriers and disadvantage that they experience.

In education, as elsewhere, this has had a strong impact; requiring, for example, steps to be taken to ensure greater access for all. This was not always the case. Following the recommendations of the 1978 Warnock Report a disabled child would be likely to be grouped by his or her education authority into one of roughly 11 categories, broadly relating to a medical or quasi-medical label, and then placed in a requisite educational setting purportedly designed to cater for their perceived 'deficit'. In many respects, such approaches have changed, and today diversity is often seen as an asset rather than a problem. Schools and colleges are encouraged, and to an extent legislatively required, to remove barriers for disabled students.

However, despite changes in policy and practice, this has rarely challenged the fabric of the way in which education is delivered to disabled students. This is explored by Anne Borsay in her chapter, locating the history of education for disabled people within a context of social oppression and measuring the progress to date and the challenges ahead with a human rights yardstick.

In many cases, the system we have inherited, whilst aiming to deliver effective educational provision for disabled students, can have the paradoxical effect of reinforcing the approach of 30 years ago. In their chapter, Cherie Booth, Marc Bush and Ruth Scott highlight this paradox, pointing out that steps taken to dismantle the rigid labelling of disabled children in favour of a rights-based approach, while maintaining a system that allocates resources in accordance with that very labelling, have entrenched the need for non-inclusive provision.

This paradox goes to the heart of the current system where a 'jigsaw of provision' framework both asserts the rights of disabled students, largely aiming towards the goal of inclusive education, and seeks to meet their needs within the established resource-based structure. This is most clearly seen in the legislation, where the 2001 Special Educational Needs and Disability Act combines the often contrasting provisions of the pre-existing resource-based special educational needs framework with the newer, rights-based Disability Discrimination Act. In his chapter, Neil Crowther argues that the current framework of the special educational needs system does not deliver the intent of greater independence for disabled students. Following Amartya Sen's 'capabilities framework', he suggests that we should instead rethink provision around a human rights-based approach.

Through each progressive stage of education, multiple layers of structure, practice, process and legislation surround and impact on disabled students. This picture and its complexity is considered by Liz Todd in her chapter, where she suggests that professionals should become aware of this context in their work. Similarly, good intentions to improve the educational experience for disabled students have often not delivered in practice, as in the area of listening to the voices of disabled students, discussed by Ann Lewis in her chapter.

Despite the positive intent of policymakers and practitioners to improve provision, concerns from parents, charities and teachers prompted successive reviews of the policy and delivery frameworks for disabled students. Most stridently, the review by the then named Education and Skills Select Committee (2006) suggested that 'the SEN system is demonstrably no longer fit for purpose and there is a need for the Government to develop a new system that puts the needs of the child at the centre of provision'. The Labour government of the day did not accept this view and the system remained. The Lamb Inquiry (DCSF, 2009), commissioned as a result of a later review by the same select committee, took a more pragmatic view, stating that 'while the aims of the SEN framework remain relevant, implementation has too often failed to live up to them'.

This evolving debate and the policy responses by successive UK governments set us a challenge as editors. As we were developing this book with our authors, a general election brought in a new and somewhat unexpected Conservative–Liberal Democrat government. At the same time, the cost of the economic shocks of the banking crisis in 2008/09 (and, so it is argued, a decade of extravagant public spending) led to a broad policy of fiscal retrenchment, with spending cuts across the public sector, placing fresh challenges on an already highly regulated and expensive area of public service provision. As editors, we sought to ensure that the essays in this volume reflect the implications of these very current issues, whilst drawing out assumptions, challenges and questions that have dominated this debate for some time.

Although not identical in approach, both Coalition partners in the new government spoke of how to implement better outcomes for disabled students in their manifestos and, as in many areas of policy, they have since sought compromise on how to resolve their differing approaches. The Coalition agreement brought together the two manifesto statements in the phrase 'We believe the most vulnerable children deserve the very highest quality of care. We will improve diagnostic assessment for school children, prevent the unnecessary closure of special schools, and remove the bias towards inclusion' (HM Government, 2010).

This statement marked a change from the previous Labour administration and their broad promotion of 'an inclusive school system', reflected in legislation, which, while not quite inclusion as many would understand it, aimed to increase the number of disabled students studying alongside their non-disabled peers. In the 2004 strategy for students with special educational needs, *Removing Barriers to Achievement* (DfES, 2004), the then government set out its view that 'All teachers should expect to teach children with special educational needs (SEN) and all schools should play their part in educating children from their local community, whatever their background or ability'.

A number of initiatives put in place by the previous administration improved outcomes for disabled students and brought together fragmented services. Alongside these, targeted policy interventions sought better coordination of support for disabled children, including *Aiming High for Disabled Children: Better Support for Families* (HM Treasury and DfES, 2007) and *The Children's Plan* (DCSF, 2007). In her chapter, Philippa Russell explores the growth of family-focused policy and considers what may come next in its development.

At the same time, the massive expansion of higher education brought successes in widening participation, including for disabled students. However, deeper issues remain, such as the complex problems of identity and access to resources, explored in a chapter by Sheila Riddell and Elisabet Weedon. Very recently, the proposed transformation of funding for higher educational institutions, set out in the Browne Review, poses key challenges for the access and participation of disabled students in higher education.

In other areas, progress has been less clear and the gap between the intent of legislation and its application to the complex arrangements of the education system has tested the boundaries of both. Applying the provisions of the Disability Discrimination Act to externally assessed qualifications, such as GCSEs and A-Levels, using structures that have existed for over a hundred years, has challenged the principles on which student progress in education is assessed. In their chapter, Olga Miller, Rory Cobb and Paul Simpson explore the opposing and apparently mutually exclusive priorities for schools: to be inclusive and yet prioritise exam results, taking the example of students with sensory impairments to illustrate their point.

The government has been swift to move towards a Green Paper, *Support and Aspiration: A New Approach to Special Educational Needs and Disability: A Consultation* (Department for Education, 2011) to consolidate its views. This restates its commitment to taking steps to equalise opportunity and seeks to address issues previously highlighted in the reviews mentioned earlier, such as supporting disabled students beyond the age of 16 and improving early assessment. In line with the political direction of the government, it seeks to devolve greater control to professionals 'on the front line' and involve the voluntary and community sector in areas such as assessments of children's needs. It also sets out plans to put parents more firmly in the driving seat, stating that 'our aim is to give parents more control over support for their child and family' (p 8) and that 'the reforms we set out in this green paper aim to provide families with confidence in, and greater control over, the services that they use and receive' (p 11). It aims to do this with measures such as the introduction of 'Education, Health and Care Plans', the option of personal budgets for families, and, in a move that will continue to provoke debate, measures to give parents 'a real choice of school' (p 5). Arriving while the reforms are taking place, we hope that the positions set out by our authors in this book will influence the development of this new policy direction.

There are clearly many issues as yet unresolved, which stretch beyond this book. How does the Conservatives' 'Big Society' marry with the direction of travel away from 'welfarism' (often considered inimical to the social model)? How might an increasing number of schools run by parents, charities and businesses serve the needs of disabled students?

From the challenge we set ourselves when this book was conceived – to explore the current state and future direction of education for disabled students in the UK – we have seen that policies, legislation and professional practice, whilst having seen some successes, have far to go to achieve better outcomes. These essays reflect the fractured experiences of schooling, a focus on exams that does not meet the needs of disabled students and the provision of support that seeks to diagnose rather than create independence.

They also show us new trends, such as cuts to public services that may bring about local divergence rather than consistent standards, and a slowing of the widening participation agenda in higher education, which may militate against the inclusion of those at the margins, particularly disabled students. For now, our last word perhaps, goes to those who take the long view of policy frameworks and political directions. Although at times polemical, Nigel Utton's chapter sets out a clear view of his personal convictions and the journey that has taken him to leading inclusive schools.

For those of us committed to the support of the social model of disability and its implications for the realisation of inclusive thinking and practice in education and society, the contradictory policy statements we are hearing are a serious and worrying development. Thus, the centrality of human rights and effective legislation is more than ever an urgent and continual necessity. The emphasis should be on the language of entitlements rather than that of needs. The importance of debate and serious discussion is essential for the development of the process of effective change. There is no room for complacency and we hope that this collection of essays will stimulate debate and provide considerable food for thought about current issues, recent developments and possible solutions.

References

DCSF (Department for Children, Schools and Families) (2007) *The Children's Plan: Building Brighter Futures,* Norwich: TSO.

DCSF (2009) *The Lamb Inquiry: Special Educational Needs and Parental Confidence*, Nottingham: DCSF Publications.

Department for Education (2011) *Support and Aspiration: A New Approach to Special Educational Needs and Disability: A Consultation,* Norwich: TSO.

DfES (Department for Education and Skills) (2004) *Removing Barriers to Achievement: The Government's Strategy for SEN*, Nottingham: DfES Publications.

Education and Skills Committee (2006) *Third Report,* www.publications. parliament.uk/pa/cm200506/cmselect/cmeduski/478/47802.htm

HM Government (2010) *The Coalition: Our Programme for Government*, London: Cabinet Office.

HM Treasury and DfES (Department for Education and Skills) (2007) *Aiming High for Disabled Children: Better Support for Families*, London: HM Treasury and DfES and Nottingham: DfES Publications.

ONE

Disability and education in historical perspective

Anne Borsay

Introduction

The human rights agenda, broadly defined, promotes health and well-being by upholding 'opportunity and choice, freedom of speech, respect for individuality and an acceptance of difference in all spheres of life' (Armstrong and Barton, 1999, p 211). For disabled people, the realisation of these aspirations is an inclusive society, where the economic, political, ideological, social and cultural barriers that underpin inequality and discrimination are dismantled. The purpose of this chapter is to assess the historical development of education for disabled children against the human rights yardstick, focusing on Britain between the late 18th century and the early 1980s. Three main themes will be pursued: the inability of legal entitlements to replace segregated with inclusive schooling; the contribution of the professions to this failure; and the threat to human rights posed by schooling that compromised participation in family, community and employment. The chapter will conclude by locating education within a broader framework of social exclusion that encompasses cultural representation as well as public policy.

From segregation to inclusion?

Charitable origins

Segregated education for disabled children dates back to the early modern period when dedicated institutions emerged from private tuition. Sensory impairments – judged to be particularly pernicious because they denied full access to the word of God – were the initial category of disability to attract attention. Thus, the first 'special' school – opened in Edinburgh in 1764 – was for deaf pupils. Although this was a commercial venture, the institutions for deaf *and* blind pupils that multiplied from the 1790s were charitable foundations, resting upon voluntary donations and subscriptions (Phillips, 2004; Borsay, 2007). From the 1840s, the same formula was applied to institutions for intellectually impaired children, inspired by the belief that 'idiocy' was no longer beyond education (Wright, 2001). The result was a network of segregated schooling. By the end of the 19th century, there were in Britain over 50 institutions for blind children; 26 for deaf children; and a National Asylum for Idiots at Earlswood in Surrey, on which four regional asylums had also been modelled (Haswell, 1876; Woodford, 2000; Wright, 2001).

The charitable ethos of these foundations was incompatible with the concept of education as a human right. First, pupils – typically aged between six and twelve – had no entitlement to a place. On the contrary, they were elected by benefactors on the basis of biographical notes that were circulated prior to electoral meetings. Second, the compassion that was used to generate funds disempowered disabled children by construing them as helpless objects of pity rather than future citizens with a right to education (Borsay, 2007). This denial of rights was compounded by the discourse of degeneration, which gathered momentum after the publication of Charles Darwin's *The Origin of Species* in 1859 and was consolidated by the formation of the Eugenics Education Society in 1907. Far from promoting education, however, the Society advocated sterilisation, marital regulation, birth control and segregation to prevent the spread of 'mental deficiency' (King, 1999).

Although all disabled people were tainted by this eugenic message, children with intellectual impairments were most directly affected. This was because a new emphasis on their untreatable condition led to the establishment of permanent institutions, committed to lifelong residence rather than the completion of a fixed-term programme of education and training. Some such foundations – like Sandlebridge Boarding School and Colony in Cheshire, which opened in 1902 – were charitable (Jackson, 2000). Far more numerically significant, however, were the local authority 'mental deficiency' institutions, which stemmed from legislation in 1913. By 1939 they were accommodating over 40,000 people (Walmsley et al, 1999), including among their inmates those incapable of being educated at school (Jones, 1972).

Statutory origins

The earlier arrival of mainstream state schooling had done little to improve the human rights of disabled children. Central government had topped up charitable general-purpose schools since the 1830s, but it was only the 1870 Education Act that authorised statutory provision to fill the gaps left by voluntary endeavour. When a decade later school attendance became compulsory for five to ten-year-olds, all children acquired the right to at least an elementary education (Harris, 2004). However, like the charitable societies whose activities it complemented, the 1870 Act was not concerned with disabled children (Tomlinson, 1982). Consequently, they were detected by default as those who had stayed at home or remained undifferentiated at school (McCoy, 1998).

Children with physical as well as sensory and intellectual impairments were caught up in this process, triggering the launch of over 40 agencies for the newly identified young 'cripples' by 1914. The charitable orthopaedic hospitals into which some of these initiatives grew during the interwar period provided a new educational destination for disabled children: the hospital school, set up to teach patients institutionalised for long periods as a result of orthopaedic surgery or the appliance of plaster casts, splints and frames (Cooter, 1993). However, the most significant outcomes of the childhood disability revealed by compulsory education arose from the Royal Commission, which reported in 1889.

Among the recommendations of the Royal Commission was schooling for blind, deaf and 'dumb' children. What drove this recommendation was the financial burden that disability imposed. Therefore, education was promoted not as a right that disabled children enjoyed by virtue of being human, but as a means of reducing pauperism (Tomlinson, 1982). In 1893, responsibility for the education of blind and deaf children was thus transferred from the poor law authorities to local education authorities (LEAs), which were given a duty to develop their own segregated schools or to grant-aid charitable schools. Six years later LEAs received enabling but not mandatory powers to provide special schools for intellectually impaired children. Not until 1918, however, was schooling for mentally *and* physically 'defective' children made compulsory (Hurt, 1988).

By the 1920s, Britain had over 500 institutions for children with sensory or physical impairments (Humphries and Gordon, 1992). The extension of the franchise, which had begun in earnest in the late 19th century, was beginning to affect the outlook of these specialist institutions whose publicity spoke in terms of preparing responsible citizens (Thomson, 1998). This 'civic' consciousness, however, was undermined by the continuing eugenic mindset, which attributed 'mental deficiency' and 'much physical deficiency' to 'poor mental endowment' (Jones, 1982, p 723). Therefore, the duty of local authorities to provide special schools for disabled children was 'inscribed within the rhetorical and ideological framework of eugenics' rather than of citizenship and human rights (Koven, 1994, p 1173).

The welfare state

This eugenic mindset was challenged by the education policy of the post-war welfare state. Reaching the statute book towards the end of the Second World War, the 1944 Education Act embraced the optimistic ethos of social reconstruction that the conflict had engendered by establishing the right of all children to a schooling suited to their 'age, aptitude and ability' (Lowe, 1993). In line with this agenda, all those 'able to benefit' from education were brought under the local authority umbrella, leaving only 'ineducable' children within the National Health Service (NHS) (Henderson, 1974). In addition, however, it was conceded that where possible disabled children were best taught in mainstream schools. Additional facilities were accordingly made available under the Handicapped Pupils and Medical Services Regulations of 1945. Therefore, as well as special attention from the teacher, disabled children in ordinary schools were to be allowed 'a favourable position in the classroom', special furniture, aids and equipment, and tuition in lip-reading if they were partially deaf (Clarke, 1951, pp 127–8).

The promise of integration implicit in these arrangements was fundamentally flawed. Special education was defined as a 'treatment' in which 'methods appropriate for persons suffering from disability of mind and/or body' were expertly applied (see the 1944 Education Act, available at: http://www.opsi.gov.uk/acts/acts1944/pdf/ukpga_19440031_en.pdf [accessed 1 September 2009]). This encouraged an essentially medical system of classification in which children were placed in one of 11 categories ranging from blind and deaf to physically handicapped and educationally subnormal. Parental choice only came into play if it was 'compatible with efficient instruction and training and the avoidance of unreasonable public expenditure'. Educational authorities – anxious to avoid any disruption to the new 'co-ordinated system of compulsory mass primary and secondary education' – were, therefore, free 'to exclude as many children as possible who might obstruct or inconvenience the smooth running of normal schools' (Tomlinson, 1982, p 50). The combined effect of these limitations was an expansion of segregated schools (Oliver, 1998; French, 2006). Consequently, despite the alleged policy of integration, the number of pupils in special schooling climbed from 38,499 in 1945 to 106,367 in 1972 (Topliss, 1975).

From the 1960s, the case for segregation was increasingly undermined by the growth of all-inclusive comprehensive education, which abandoned selection by ability at the age of 11. At the same time, the debate about integrating disabled children was advancing. An early sign was the transfer of junior training centres for children deemed 'ineducable' from the NHS to LEAs in 1970 (Fulcher, 1989). However, the most significant development was the 1981 Education Act. Drawing on the 1978 Warnock Report, the Act dropped medical classification and the concept of educational treatment and replaced them with 'special educational needs', which was defined as 'having a learning difficulty which calls for special educational provision'. There were two constructions of learning difficulty: having 'a significantly greater difficulty in learning than the majority of children of his [sic] age'; or having a 'disability which either prevents or hinders ... making use of educational facilities of a kind generally provided in schools' (see the 1981 Education Act, available at: http://www.opsi.gov.uk/acts/acts1981/pdf/ukpga_19810060_en.pdf [accessed 1 September 2009]).

Although these two definitions were intended to replace the categorisation of disabled children with 'a continuum of need', they merely produced a change of terminology as medical classification gave way to three bands of learning difficulty: moderate, severe and profound and multiple (Swain et al, 2003, p 126). Moreover, neither definition acknowledged Warnock's contention that special educational needs were relative, or dependent upon the physical and social environment of the school; as the report elaborated: 'Schools differ, often widely, in outlook, expertise, resources, accommodation, organization and physical and social surroundings', and so it is 'impossible to establish precise criteria for defining what constitutes handicap' (Warnock, 1978, p 37). The monies to adapt these varying environments were not guaranteed because the obligation to accommodate disabled children in mainstream schools was again conditional upon 'the efficient education' of other children and the efficient use of resources. Therefore, although the 1981 Act aspired to reduce the number of disabled children in segregated schooling, it did not facilitate the inclusive education essential to human rights in which mainstream classrooms became accessible.

Medicine, psychology and teaching

Medicine, psychology and teaching – the occupational groups who competed for professional kudos within the sphere of special schooling – were implicated in its failure to deliver inclusive education. The first institutions for blind and deaf children specifically ruled out medical intervention and insisted that pupils were admitted for educational purposes only (Borsay, 2005). The teachers offering this instruction were initially of low status with poor wages, long hours and spartan residential facilities (Beaver, 1992). In the second half of the 19th century, however, they began to organise to protect their interests. Command of the communication skills used to educate children with sensory impairments was critical to this process. Therefore, after 1880 ambitious teachers seized on the conclusion of the infamous Milan Congress that 'only oral instruction could fully restore deaf people to society' (Lane, 1993, pp 113–14). Its imposition contributed to the professionalisation of deaf education by identifying teachers with the dominant linguistic culture and denigrating or excluding those who practised sign language. At a time, though, when three quarters of British schools supported this manual method rather than the oral method or a combination of the two (Branson and Miller, 2000), the effect was to deny deaf pupils the right to talk in the language of their choice.

Although the early blind and deaf institutions resisted medicine, doctors were later to play a central role in the management of special education. Learning difficulty came under medical control from the mid-19th century with doctors dominating the new 'idiot' asylums. John Langdon Down was medical superintendent at Earlswood between 1858 and 1868. Whilst there, he not only 'classified a new type of mental disability' – named Down's syndrome in his honour – but also 'pioneered the medical treatment of "idiocy"' (Wright, 2001). Drugs were part of this treatment, but Langdon Down also applied a moral method of instruction, based on rewards and punishments. This embryonic form of behaviour modification was employed within an existing programme of physical activity, designed to improve the mind by disciplining the unruly movements of the body (Wright, 2001, p 199). Similar programmes, comprising drill and gymnastics, were adopted in blind and deaf institutions with games, dancing and swimming added to the repertoire to discipline the effects of sensory impairment (Borsay, 2005).

Medical intervention in special education went beyond the endorsement of physical exercise to include intrusive treatments. One of the more recent manifestations is the controversial cochlear implant

(Hogan, 1998), but medical technologies were also a problem in the past. Children with partial sight, for instance, found that the contact lenses developed in the 1950s were awkward and painful to use, despite the enthusiasm surrounding their arrival (French, 2006). Furthermore, orthopaedic institutions like the Heritage Craft Schools and Hospital at Chailey in Sussex had ambitious plans to remould the disabled child, medical treatment featuring as one element within a package that also included education, vocational training and leisure (Koven, 1994). Yet many of the cumbersome aids fitted to thalidomide children resident in the 1960s impeded rather than enhanced their functioning (Medus, 2009). In closed environments, however, it was difficult for children or parents either to complain about the institutional regime, or to demand non-interference, against the power of the medical establishment.

With the advent of state education from the 1890s, doctors became increasingly involved in the assessment as well as the management and treatment of disabled children. Their vehicle was the local authority School Medical Service, founded in 1907 with a statutory duty to inspect children's health (Harris, 2004). The Board of Education regarded the Service as pivotal to the expansion of special schooling (Thomson, 1998). Doctors were soon joined by psychologists following the introduction of the IQ test as an assessment tool. Gillian Sutherland has argued that this test had benign potential because it identified a continuum of ability that stretched from the normal to the abnormal and hence discredited segregation (Sutherland, 1984). By the 1920s, however, 'Psychologists, through mental testing procedures, were acquiring the power to legitimate the removal of large numbers of children from normal education' (Tomlinson, 1982, p 48).

Despite the reliance on the IQ test, doctors continued to lead the 'ascertainment' of physically and mentally impaired children after the 1944 Act. Thirty years later, psychologists had achieved parity, as evidenced by the additional report that they were now required to provide for the assessment process (Russell, 1978; Tomlinson, 1982). This new-found power was not rooted in more reliable testing, and, although the measurement of IQ continued to discriminate against *all* children by failing to recognise the effects of social background (Lowe, 1993), disabled children were further disadvantaged. Rather than blurring the normal–abnormal boundary, testing firmed up the deviance of those with intellectual impairments. Moreover, as the Board of Education had recognised as long ago as 1936, to 'apply the ordinary tests of intelligence to a child who is defective in sight or in hearing is to do him [sic] serious injustice' (Hurt, 1988, p 164). On both grounds, therefore, psychology justified the special school by supplying spurious scientific criteria for demarcation. In consequence, with this institution ensconced, segregation became an all too easy means for not only regulating any 'disruptive' behaviour, but also reducing tolerance of difference (Tomlinson, 1982). School exclusions subsequently took on this role, as new categories of disturbing behaviour (like Attention Deficit Disorder) were increasingly medicalised and responsibility was increasingly located with children or their 'inadequate' families rather than the educational system (Armstrong and Barton, 1999).

The 1981 Act's concept of special educational needs, which sought to capture this diversity, strengthened the professional standing of teachers by ceasing to construe education as a treatment in the domain of medicine or psychology. However, the model of professionalisation advanced was a bureaucratic and not substantive one. Scant attention was thus paid to how the curriculum might aggravate the difficulties of disabled children; and the skills to teach them remained the preserve of in-service training, a post-qualification add-on rather than an intrinsic part of the syllabus. Conversely, the bureaucratic process of 'statementing' was championed as teachers became heavily involved in the multi-professional assessments that released special provision (Fulcher, 1989). However, only a minority of disabled children – those with more serious special educational needs – were actually 'statemented'. Integration rather than inclusion was the goal (French, 2006). Furthermore, while consultation was compulsory, LEAs were not obliged to obtain parental approval and parents had only limited rights of appeal to a local committee, which was authorised to ask for reconsideration but not to overrule a decision (Fulcher, 1989). Even the Special Education Needs and Disability Tribunal (now Panel), set up later under the 1993 Education Act and independent of local authorities, had on its own admission 'quite limited' powers, which were restricted to demanding an assessment or a statement where one was refused or insisting on alterations to the statement's content. If disability discrimination was proved, reasonable action to remedy it could be ordered, though not financial compensation. The Tribunal/Panel did produce a guide for children and young people (www.sendist.gov.uk). However, the dominance of the professions undermined both them and their families in the determination of provision and, in any event, their own requirements were not guaranteed by parental involvement. Consequently, the dominance of the professions disempowered families in the determination of needs (Oliver, 1996) and the requirements of disabled children were not guaranteed by parental involvement where there was a conflict of interest (Oliver, 1998) – for example, a preference for social training (Glendinning, 1983). Therefore, the victory of the teaching profession over medicine and psychology did not ensure that human rights in education were protected.

Family, community and employment

Despite the human rights deficiencies, by no means all educational experiences were negative. Alice – educated after 1981 – who became deaf as a baby due to meningitis, had a positive experience of mainstream education at both primary and secondary level. Although the school was not designed for deaf pupils and had no visual alarms or electronic displays, she was supported through a deaf unit where teachers 'made sure I got on well with the work and mixed with hearing people' but also taught her sign language and introduced her to the Deaf community. Consequently, she remained comfortable about going 'into both worlds' (Jasvinder et al, 2008, pp 123–4). Disabled children were also happily absorbed into mainstream education before the 1980 Act took effect, including migrants from special schools; and not all those who were segregated expressed dissatisfaction (Madge and Fassam, 1982). Moreover, even where institutional regimes were harsh and punishments were brutal, friendships were sustaining (Humphries and Gordon, 1992; French with Swain, 2000; Cook et al, 2001).

Yet whatever the quality of their internal relationships, schools that forced pupils to board denied them the sense of inclusion that Alice enjoyed and restricted their right to participate in family life, the local community and employment. The late Victorian commentator D.O. Haswell lambasted this exile. Writing with particular reference to blind institutions, he complained that they intensified the visual incarceration already inflicted on blind people and subjected them to a regime that not only failed to develop their abilities, but also weakened their physical and mental health (Haswell, 1876). Conversely, many early 20th-century reformers – under the influence of eugenic thinking – welcomed the removal of disabled children whose parents were poor, blaming the impoverished home environment for endangering morality as well as causing impairment. By the early 1950s, however, the Chief Medical Officer was declaring that: 'A child should never be removed from home unless it is quite certain that there is no practicable alternative' because the family was 'the fundamental basis for the child's emotional development and security' (French, 2006, p 124).

Disabled children's experiences of segregation testify to the force of this argument. The pain of initial desertion was acute; and if returning after the school holidays was hard, so was going home. Indeed, it was 'more traumatic … because, although in your head you knew about mothers, grandmothers and whoever, these people were basically strangers to you' (French, 2006, pp 182–3). Long distances aggravated this alienation. Some children were able to see their parents only once a year, but even where families were nearby, face-to-face contact was discouraged and visits allowed just once a month. Access to community participation was also limited. Not only were special schools often isolated from local neighbourhoods, but the children who attended them were also acutely conscious of their difference and hence had difficulty in forging friendships during holidays or weekends at home. Though their loneliness may have eased when day schools became more common in the 1970s, there was still the stigma of the special school bus (Oswin, 1978; Campbell and Oliver, 1996; French, 2006). Consequently, it was disabled children educated with their non-disabled peers who mixed most frequently with school friends out of school (Madge and Fassam, 1982).

In addition to eroding rights to family and community engagement, segregated schooling put at risk disabled children's employment opportunities in adult life. The reason was low expectations. From the first days of the blind and deaf institutions, the formal curriculum was combined with vocational training, which reinforced the divisions of class and gender: boys were engaged in workshops learning how to make baskets, mats, clothing and boots; girls were engaged in institutional housework, learning how to wash, clean and sew (Borsay, 2005). The preoccupation with manual skills, which extended to all disabled children and endured into the post-war period, discouraged schools from entering pupils for public examinations (Barnes et al, 1999). Therefore, in the early 1970s, a national survey revealed that 60% of impaired men and women had no formal qualifications or skills – compared with 47% of the population as a whole (Buckle, 1971).

This shortage of educational credentials curtailed employment opportunities in adulthood. True, the post-war period saw a severing of the link between the special school and workshop, which had so invidiously portrayed manual labour as the natural destination for disabled children. At the same time, a raft of policy measures was introduced, including the notorious quota scheme that was so inept in compelling larger employers to recruit 3% of their workforce from the disabled population (Jordan, 1979). However, careers advice was poor and job opportunities remained typecast, as being a typist, telephonist or piano tuner replaced the traditional craft occupations. Some individuals escaped: for example, David, who became a basket maker in the late 1950s, was subsequently employed as a home teacher of blind people, a computer programmer and a social welfare officer (French, 2006).

Overall, however, disabled people were concentrated at the bottom of the labour market and exposed to high unemployment. Therefore, in a study of children born during one week in 1958, 22% of those ascertained as 'handicapped' under the 1944 Education Act had taken a first job that was unskilled, compared with 9% of all 15- to 24-year-olds. Two thirds of this 'handicapped' group had experienced unemployment: twice as many as the 'non-handicapped' group (Walker, 1982).

Of course, segregated schools were not alone in denying the right to well-paid, secure employment. In a society where discrimination against disabled people was rampant, they were just one conduit for transmitting deep-seated prejudices rooted in bodily perfection and full economic productivity. Therefore, for Jock Young – a pupil at the Glasgow Deaf and Dumb Institution in the 1930s – the employer was the obstacle: 'they wouldn't take me because of my deafness and I was sent to cobblers' workshops employing deaf people. Deaf people could get jobs as joiners, painters, and cobblers, but I wanted to be an electrical engineer' (Hutchinson, 2007, p 273). Nevertheless, by removing disabled children from everyday social interaction, special schools compounded the negative attitudes that frustrated the achievement of an inclusive society with the full spectrum of human rights.

Conclusion

This chapter has evaluated the development of education policies for disability; explored the contributions of doctors, psychologists and teachers to their shortcomings; and examined access to family, community and work. The segregated system that evolved from the late 18th century prevented disabled children from obtaining the full rights of citizenship. This exclusion was multifaceted. As the American political theorist Iris Young has argued, social oppression may involve violence, powerlessness, marginalisation, exploitation and cultural imperialism. Historically, disabled education was guilty on all five counts. First, disabled children were subjected to physical and psychological violence at school. Second, both they and their families were powerless to influence the school environment. Third, this school environment marginalised pupils in and excluded them from mainstream education, their families and local communities, and the labour market. Fourth, it left them prone to economic exploitation in an economy that rewarded educational qualifications. Finally, the special school fed cultural imperialism: 'the paradox of experiencing oneself as invisible at the same time that one is marked out as different' (Young, 1990, p 60). By separating disabled children, segregation ensured that the experience of disability remained remote from non-disabled people. Consequently, what it was like to be disabled found little expression in the dominant culture because literature and the visual arts reproduced stereotyped images that sustained isolation.

The task of the historian is to analyse the past because the changing context in which human experiences occur make predicting the future impossible. Nevertheless, the broad-ranging social oppression perpetrated by education policies in previous centuries does not bode well for social inclusion today. In the 1995 Disability Discrimination Act (DDA), education was exempt. Six years later the 2001 Special Educational Needs and Disability Act did make it unlawful for schools to discriminate against disabled children and this requirement was strengthened by the extension of the DDA to education in 2005. However, neither piece of legislation was sufficiently ambitious to allow children to bring a case in their own right and the implementation of both Acts continues to be frustrated by budgetary constraints, professional shortcomings and prejudicial attitudes towards disability. History suggests that such barriers to the educational rights of disabled children will be slow to break down.

References

Armstrong, F. and Barton, L. (1999) '"Is There Anyone There Concerned with Human Rights?" Cross-Cultural Connections, Disability and the Struggle for Change in England', in F. Armstrong and L. Barton (eds) *Disability, Human Rights and Education: Cross-Cultural Perspectives*, Buckingham: Open University Press, pp 210–29.

Barnes, C., Mercer, G. and Shakespeare, T. (1999) *Exploring Disability: A Sociological Introduction*, Cambridge: Polity.

Beaver, P. (1992) *A Tower of Strength: Two Hundred Years of the Royal School for Deaf Children, Margate*, Lewes: The Book Guild.

Borsay, A. (2005) *Disability and Social Policy in Britain since 1750: A History of Exclusion*, Basingstoke: Palgrave Macmillan.

Borsay, A. (2007) 'Deaf Children and Charitable Education in Britain, 1790–1944', in A. Borsay and P. Shapely (eds) *Medicine, Charity and Mutual Aid: The Consumption of Health and Welfare in Britain, c. 1550–1950*, Aldershot: Ashgate, pp 71–90.

Branson, J. and Miller, D. (2000) 'From Myth to History: Maginn, Gallaudet and the Destruction of the BSL-Based Manualism in Deaf Education in Britain', *Deaf History Journal*, vol 4, no 1, pp 7–17.

Buckle, J.R. (1971) *Work and Housing of Impaired Persons in Great Britain*, London: HMSO.

Campbell, J. and Oliver, M. (1996) *Disability Politics: Understanding Our Past, Changing Our Future*, London: Routledge.

Clarke, J.S. (1951) *Disabled Citizens*, London: Allen and Unwin.

Cook, T., Swain, J. and French, S. (2001) 'Voices from Segregated Schooling: Towards an Inclusive Education System', *Disability and Society*, vol 16, no 2, pp 293–310.

Cooter, R. (1993) *Surgery and Society in Peace and War: Orthopaedics and the Organization of Modern Medicine, 1880–1948*, Basingstoke: Macmillan.

Darwin, C. (1996 [1859]) *The Origin of Species*, ed. by G. Beer, Oxford: Oxford University Press.

French, S. (2006) *An Oral History of the Education of Visually Impaired People*, Lewiston, Queenston and Lampeter: Edwin Mellen Press.

French, S. with Swain, J. (2000) 'Institutional Abuse: Memories of a "Special" School for Visually Impaired Girls – a Personal Account', in J. Bornat, R. Perks, P. Thompson and J. Walmsley (eds) *Oral History, Health and Welfare*, London: Routledge, pp 159–79.

Fulcher, G. (1989) *Disabling Policies? A Comparative Approach to Education Policy and Disability*, London, New York and Philadelphia: Falmer Press.

Glendinning, C. (1983) *Unshared Care: Parents and Their Disabled Children*, London: Routledge and Kegan Paul.

Harris, B. (2004) *The Origins of the British Welfare State: Social Welfare in England and Wales, 1800–1945*, Basingstoke: Palgrave Macmillan.

Haswell, D.O. (1876) *The Social Condition of the Blind*, published by the author.

Henderson, P. (1974) *Disability in Childhood and Youth*, Oxford: Oxford University Press.

Hogan, A. (1998) 'Carving out a Space to Act: Acquired Impairment and Contested Identity', *Health*, vol 2, no 1, pp 75–90.

Humphries, S. and Gordon, P. (1992) *Out of Sight: The Experience of Disability 1900–1950*, Plymouth: Northcote House.

Hurt, J.S. (1988) *Outside the Mainstream: A History of Special Education*, London: Batsford.

Hutchinson, I. (2007) *A History of Disability in Nineteenth-Century Scotland*, Lewiston, Queenston and Lampeter: Edwin Mellen Press.

Jackson, M. (2000) *The Borderland of Imbecility: Medicine, Society and the Fabrication of the Feeble Mind in Late Victorian and Edwardian England*, Manchester: Manchester University Press.

Jasvinder, Arlene, Geoff and Alice (2008) 'Disabled People's Testimonies', in J. Swain and S. French (eds) *Disability on Equal Terms*, London: Sage Publications, pp 115–26.

Jones, G. (1982) 'Eugenics and Social Policy between the Wars', *Historical Journal*, vol 25, no 3, pp 717–28.

Jones, K. (1972) *A History of the Mental Health Services*, London: Routledge and Kegan Paul.

Jordan, D. (1979) *A New Employment Programme Wanted for Disabled People*, London: Disability Alliance.

King, D. (1999) *In the Name of Liberalism: Illiberal Social Policy in the United States and Britain*, Oxford: Oxford University Press.

Koven, S. (1994) 'Remembering and Dismemberment: Crippled Children, Wounded Soldiers, and the Great War in Great Britain', *American Historical Review*, vol 99, no 4, pp 1167–202.

Lane, H. (1993) *The Mask of Benevolence: Disabling the Deaf Community*, New York: Vintage.

Lowe, R. (1993) *The Welfare State in Britain since 1945*, Basingstoke: Macmillan.

Madge, N. and Fassam, M. (1982) *Ask the Children: Experiences of Physical Disability in the School Years*, London: Batsford.

McCoy, L. (1998) 'Education for Labour: Social Problems of Nationhood', in G. Lewis (ed) *Forming Nation, Framing Welfare*, London: Routledge, pp 93–138.

Medus, L. (2009) *No Hand to Hold and No Legs to Dance on: Laughing and Loving – a Thalidomide Survivor's Story*, Bedlinog, Mid-Glamorgan: Accent Press.

Oliver, M. (1996) *Understanding Disability: From Theory to Practice*, Basingstoke: Macmillan.

Oliver, M. (1998) 'The Social and Political Context of Education Policy: The Case of Special Needs', in L. Barton (ed) *The Politics of Special Educational Needs*, London, New York and Philadelphia: Falmer Press, pp 13–31.

Oswin, M. (1978) *Holes in the Welfare Net*, London: Bedford Square Press.

Phillips, G. (2004) *The Blind in British Society: Charity, State and Community, c.1780–1930*, Aldershot: Ashgate.

Russell, P. (1978) *The Wheelchair Child*, London: Souvenir Press.

Sutherland, G. (1984) *Ability, Merit and Measurement: Mental Testing and English Education, 1880–1940*, Oxford: Clarendon Press.

Swain, J., French, S. and Cameron, C. (2003) *Controversial Issues in a Disabling Society*, Buckingham: Open University Press.

Thomson, M. (1998) *The Problem of Mental Deficiency: Eugenics, Democracy, and Social Policy in Britain, c.1870–1959*, Oxford: Clarendon Press.

Tomlinson, S. (1982) *A Sociology of Special Education*, London: Routledge and Kegan Paul.

Topliss, E. (1975) *Provision for the Disabled*, Oxford and London: Basil Blackwell and Martin Robertson.

Walker, A. (1982) *Unqualified and Underemployed: Handicapped Young People and the Labour Market*, Basingstoke: Macmillan.

Walmsley, J., Atkinson, D. and Rolph, S. (1999) 'Community Care and Mental Deficiency, 1913 to 1945', in P. Bartlett and D. Wright (eds) *Outside the Walls of the Asylum: A History of Care in the Community, 1750–2000*, London: Athlone, pp 181–203.

Warnock, M. (1978) *Special Educational Needs: Report of the Committee of Enquiry into the Education of Handicapped Children and Young People*, Cmnd 7212, London: HMSO.

Woodford, D.E. (2000) *Touch, Touch and Touch Again*, Feltham, Middlesex: British Deaf History Society.

Wright, D. (2001) *Mental Disability in Victorian England: The Earlswood Asylum 1847–1901*, Oxford: Clarendon Press.

Young, I.M. (1990) *Justice and the Politics of Difference*, Princeton, NJ: Princeton University Press.

TWO

Complex needs, divergent frameworks: challenges disabled children face in accessing appropriate support services and inclusive educational opportunities

Cherie Booth, Marc Bush and Ruth Scott[1]

Introduction

In May 2010, the new Coalition government published its *Programme for Government* (HM Government, 2010). In it, the government states that it will 'prevent the unnecessary closure of special schools, and remove the bias towards inclusion' (p 29). This claim is based on two core beliefs; first, that the previous government's decision to close special schools was unnecessary; and, second, that the outgoing administration had created, in policy and practice, a bias towards mainstream education.

During the 2010 election campaign these two policy assumptions were placed in the lap of the Prime Minister-to-be, the Rt Hon David Cameron MP. Whilst out on the election trail he was approached by Jonathan Bartley, a South London parent of a disabled child, who had had to fight extremely hard to get his son into a mainstream school.[2] Mr Bartley questioned the party leader about a statement in the Conservative manifesto that suggested they wanted to reverse an 'ideological bias' towards inclusive education (Conservative Party, 2010). He claimed that his son's experience clearly demonstrated that there is no bias towards inclusive mainstream education, but rather a bias towards special school provision.

Mr Cameron's response was to talk about the difficulty that parents currently experienced in getting the choice of school that they wanted for their child. His aspiration seemed to be that a reformed system could bring about real parental choice that could lead to effective provision irrespective of 'whether it is [in a] special school or whether it is [in a] mainstream [one]'. He placed emphasis on the notion that the fulfilment of parental choice about an educational placement would be a marker of an appropriate, responsive and effective system.

Clearly, both Mr Cameron and Mr Bartley agreed on the point that the system currently does not work for parents, does not serve their choice and ultimately can lead to disabled children being placed in inappropriate educational services. Where they differed was the direction in which the bias was travelling. In this chapter, we will argue that, in part, both Mr Bartley and Mr Cameron were correct in their assertions. Mr Cameron was right that there was an ideological approach to inclusive education; however, we would argue that this is more in the sense that the last government's policy belied practice in this area. He was also right in the claim that in the current system parental choice is undermined by the way in which policy frameworks and legislation are structured. We will, however, suggest that the structural bias is, as Mr Bartley argues, towards specialist and typically segregated education for disabled children.

Our discussion will demonstrate that this bias towards special schools is due to the complex relationship that has evolved between children's education and social care law. In our analysis, which covers England and Wales, we will show how the policy and legislative frameworks of education and social care, over the last two decades in particular, have taken divergent approaches, which has restricted the progress of inclusive education. It is at this point that we will avoid the narration of the long and tedious debates surrounding the definition of inclusive education by providing our own. By inclusive education, the authors mean the effective and sustainable provision of education, care and support to a disabled child in a mainstream environment, where the student has a tailored curriculum that enables them to learn and socialise alongside their non–disabled peers. When we refer to the concept of inclusion and inclusive education in this chapter it is this characterisation that we are discussing.

Complex needs, divergent frameworks

We hope that the discussion in this chapter will achieve three specific outcomes. The first is to stimulate further debate on these issues amongst students, parents, providers, academics and practising professionals. The second is to inform the forthcoming debates that will arise on these issues. The Green Paper *Support and Aspiration: A New Approach to Special Educational Needs and Disability: A Consultation* (Department for

Education, 2011) makes clear the government's intention that 'There should be real choice for parents and that is why we are committed to removing any bias towards inclusion that obstructs parent choice and preventing the unnecessary closure of special schools'. We hope that this chapter and the subsequent debate it stimulates will provide a greater insight to policymakers about the realities of parents' and children's experiences of a system that is biased towards special school education.

The final outcome is to give hope to parents of disabled children and practitioners working with them that an inclusive and sustainable solution can be reached if people sufficiently understand the direction and failures of the current system. This is important not least because of the projected increase in the number of children with SEN entering our education system. There are approximately 770,000 disabled children (IPPR, 2007) and 1.6 million children with SEN (Audit Commission, 2002) under the age of 16, living in Britain. It is predicted that the number of disabled children will increase to 1.25 million by 2029 (IPPR, 2007). Advances in medical science have meant that many more disabled children born with complex impairments are reaching adulthood (HM Treasury/DfES, 2007), and recent projections (Emerson, 2009) have indicated that, for children below the age of seven, the prevalence of complex learning difficulties will continue to rise by 4.8% each year. Consequently, the next 10 years are likely to see a steady rise in the number of families with disabled children who have complex needs and require significant levels of service and support. To reflect this, the focus of our discussion will be children who require social care and support in their everyday school lives, and their parents.

Disabled children with complex needs highlight an important tension between social care, education policy and the law. They transcend traditional distinctions between care and curricular support. Some disabled children require medical support in school or help with meeting physical needs such as eating or going to the toilet. Meeting the physical, health and education requirements of a child with complex needs in a mainstream educational environment is seen by some as difficult, and in a large number of cases the outcome is a placement in a special school. This is often as much a consequence of the way the law has developed over the last 30 years as it is a result of practical considerations based on education and social care needs.

Policy and legislation relating to disabled children have broadly developed in the three core areas of education, care and disability discrimination. The result has been the emergence of parallel approaches to provision for children. In education, the law takes a resource-blind, rights-based approach, and in care, the law takes a resource-led approach, which balances the entitlement to support services with the pressures on local care budgets. Disability discrimination law, as enacted, gives both positive and negative rights. Each individual has the right not to be discriminated against and, at the same time, to have reasonable adjustments made to enable their full participation in society so that they are not placed at a disadvantage. Finally the 1998 Human Rights Act has had an impact on this area in that it prohibits public authorities from interfering with, amongst other things, family life[3] and education.[4]

None of these different legal paths are without difficulties, and the overall impact of the divergent legal options is problematic and fragmented, with each approach having its own weaknesses and complexities. As a result, case law in this area often takes a nuanced approach, trying to make sense of the inherent difficulties in reconciling the legislation from both local authorities' and parents' perspectives. It is this tension and its roots in a systematic bias towards special school education that we will examine in the subsequent sections of this chapter.

Section 1: The development of SEN law and policy

Mainstream education for all?

Since the Warnock Report (HM Government, 1978), there has been a policy assumption that while local authorities should make provision for children with SEN in mainstream schools, disabled children with complex needs require a special school placement. This is because the mainstream education infrastructure remains unable to meet fully the curricular and care needs of this group of children. More recent initiatives such as 'Building Schools for the Future'[5] have failed to substantially address these access barriers.

The Warnock Committee[6] suggested that of the 20% of students with SEN, 2% might have support needs that went beyond what mainstream provision could provide at the time. Despite much debate between opponents and proponents, almost three decades later this sentiment remains. A government strategy from 2004 (DfES, 2004), like the Warnock Report before it, asserts that special school provision should still be used for those children with complex needs, reflecting the UNESCO Salamanca Statement and framework on SEN (UNESCO, 1994).

More recently, the Labour government made a stronger statement about the right to inclusive education by inserting an interpretative reservation[7] on Article 24, Clause 2(a) and (b) of the UN Convention on the Rights of Persons with Disabilities (CRPD). The interpretative declaration clarifies the previous administration's understanding of the definition of *inclusive education* in the CRPD to include both mainstream and special school provision. This is despite the fact that many disabled children with complex needs thrive in a mainstream environment learning alongside their peers.

This assertion was embedded into legislation, at the recommendation of the Warnock Committee, in the 1981 Education Act.[8] The Act introduced the legal requirement for local education authorities (LEAs) to identify and assess pupils with SEN and provide suitable educational provision. The 1981 Act was replaced by the 1993 Education Act, which was subsequently consolidated into the 1996 Education Act. The 1993 Education Act (now set out in Part IV of the 1996 Education Act) required the Secretary of State for Education to issue a code of practice on SEN. This code of practice was to give practical guidance to LEAs and the governing bodies of all state schools about their responsibilities for all children with SEN. This created a disproportionate reliance on a Statement by parents seeking options for their children's education.

Statement of SEN

A Statement of SEN is the core document of entitlement for children with complex educational needs. LEAs were required to identify and assess children for SEN, make a Statement of SEN and then, crucially, make provision for the child as specified in the Statement. In accordance with the Act, the Statement gives general information about the child, a description of the assessment of the child's needs and what provision will be put in place to meet this need. It further specifies what school or type of school the child should attend and outlines how any non-educational needs will be met through provision.

After a draft Statement has been made, the child's parents have 15 days to comment on it and say which school (or type of school) they want their child to attend. If parents feel that the final Statement does not reflect the needs or best interests of their child they can appeal against the Statement.[9] The 1993 Education Act (now under the provisions of the 1996 Education Act) established a national SEN Tribunal, which hears parents' appeals against the decisions of the LEA about the child's SEN provision. The recently published Lamb Inquiry (DCSF, 2009a) into parental confidence in the SEN system recommends that parents be given a right to appeal a decision not to amend a Statement following an annual or interim review, and that the right to appeal to the Tribunal be extended to children and young people. The Labour government had indicated that it was minded to implement these recommendations, but at the time of writing the Coalition government has not made any formal commitment.

The Statement of SEN has become of central importance in the system. It is important as, if used effectively, it is a legally enforceable document of entitlement. However, since the LEA is responsible for both the assessment and funding of Statements under the Education Acts, in practice, the system has an inbuilt incentive for the LEA to minimise the child's rights under a Statement, as it is the LEA's resources that will have to be spent to meet the child's need. Much of the subsequent appeal process, if activated at all, concentrates on ensuring that a fair balance is struck between the interests of the child on the one hand, and the associated cost of provision to LEAs on the other.[10] This is a situation that frequently leaves parents and children with insufficient resources to meet their educational and care needs. Soundings from the new Coalition government indicate that this is an area they would review to reform the cohabitation of the assessor and funder of Statements.

Reducing the reliance on Statements

The government's strategy on SEN published in 2004 shifted the emphasis of provision away from a reliance on Statements and focused on devolving funding and provision responsibilities from local authorities to schools (DfES, 2004). The rationale for the reduced reliance on Statements was that increased delegation of SEN funding to schools would lead to faster local action on inclusive provision. However, the reduction in the use of Statements has led to the lack of a legal document of entitlement, which has placed parents of disabled children in a precarious and vulnerable position.

In situations where no agreement can be reached between the school and parents about appropriate SEN provision, parents no longer have a legal document (SEN Statement) to assert their right to provision, nor do they have access to the effective mechanisms for conflict resolution that a Statement provides. As a consequence, many disabled children do not receive the appropriate level of support or curricular access in order to participate meaningfully in education. In turn, this leads many parents who want a Statement for their child to opt for a special school place, which brings with it a Statement and the whole framework of rights, including an appeal to the Tribunal, thus fuelling a false preference for the special school option.

Families describe a range of new challenges that arise from the reduction in the use of Statements. They find that when they move from one authority to another without a Statement, it is extremely difficult to compel the new authority to provide the same level of resources that had been provided by the school in the old authority. In the majority of cases, this leads to a placement, even if only temporarily, in an inappropriate special school or in the worse cases no educational placement at all.

Following the recommendations of the Lamb Inquiry (DCSF, 2009a), the 2010 Children, Schools and Families Act amended the 1996 Education Act by introducing a right to appeal when a local authority refuses to amend a Statement after an annual review.[11] However, the effectiveness of this new legislation will be undermined if more LEAs reduce their reliance on Statements.

Disability discrimination

More recently the remit of the independent Tribunal was extended under Part 2, Section 17 of the 2001 Special Educational Needs and Disability Act (SENDA). The newly founded Special Educational Needs and Disability Tribunal (SENDIST)[12] was now able to consider disability discrimination. The introduction of protection from disability discrimination into education law – through SENDA – brought with it the positive and negative rights framework adopted in the 1995 Disability Discrimination Act.[13] Under this new legal framework, LEAs and schools have positive duties (in addition to the Disability Equality Duty) to make reasonable adjustments (DfES, 2001), ensure protection from discrimination in the admission to schools and guarantee access to curricular activity.[14] This was extended under the 2010 Equality Act, which put a duty on schools and local authorities to provide auxiliary aids as a reasonable adjustment. For disabled children this strengthened previous rights–based international, regional and domestic legal frameworks outlining equity in access to education.[15] Moreover, it created a new focus for legal redress in SEN provision.

The Disability Equality Duty (DED)[16] is (within discrimination law) both a positive and proactive perspective and an effective way of challenging the problems and conflicts that arise within the current legal framework on a local authority level. Judicial interpretation is still in the early stages, but the DED can be a powerful tool to address fundamental problems in policy and the implementation of these areas of law beyond individual concerns.[17] Often the DED addresses process and, although procedure can affect results, it sometimes does not have the impact desired in terms of addressing systemic concerns. However, the DED should be an important part of any legal challenge going forward and may offer cumulatively the best avenue to challenge overarching policy and practice rather than individual decisions.[18] This is strengthened in the new Public Sector Equality Duty provided in the 2010 Equality Act.

The consequence of the new provisions under SENDA was a surge in the use of disability discrimination legislation in an attempt to ensure appropriate provision for disabled children through the Tribunal system.[19] However, the increased use of disability discrimination legislation may not be the most effective way of improving SEN provision for disabled children. Redress under SENDA focuses on how existing resources can ensure equal access to education for disabled children, rather than the enforcement of a SEN Statement, which can require LEAs to commit new resources and provision into the system. At a time where local budgets are being cut, there will be less resources for local authorities to draw upon, making special school education the most financially convenient solution for local authorities and the only feasible option for parents.

Further, the use of disability discrimination legislation, in particular the interpretation of more favourable treatment, has been recently weakened by a judgment in a housing case in the House of Lords. In *London Borough of Lewisham v Malcolm*,[20] the House of Lords changed the legal interpretation of what constitutes a comparator in discrimination.[21] More recently the Court of Appeal held that this decision applies in the educational context.[22] Prior to the *Malcolm* cases, the comparator (the person to whom the potentially discriminated disabled child should be compared) in an education case would have been a non-disabled pupil who, for example, did not behave in the same way as the disabled pupil, as it was assumed that the reason for the disabled pupil's behaviour was related to their impairment or condition. After the *Malcolm* judgment, the comparator has changed to a non-disabled pupil who behaved in the same way as the disabled pupil. The pre-*Malcolm* comparator was, however, re-established in the debate surrounding and enactment of the 2010 Equality Act.

Section 2: The development of care law and policy for disabled children and their families

The chapter thus far has discussed how the development of education law, in relation to disabled children, has formed a legal system that implicitly favours segregated education for disabled children. This is mainly due to the assertion that the current education system cannot meet the needs of disabled children effectively, in particular those with complex needs. Additionally, this systemic inability to meet the needs of disabled children and their families in an inclusive way is mirrored in the development of social care and support legislation (PWC, 2006).

Who cares about eligibility?

Whereas the basis of legal development around education is characterised by rights, social care and support legislation for disabled children focuses on entitlement and eligibility for services. This framework is based on the introduction of the 1948 National Assistance Act (NAA),[23] which put responsibility on local authorities to provide accommodation and services to disabled people and created a duty to carry out an assessment of need for anyone who might require residential care.

This was supplemented with the introduction of the 1970 Chronically Sick and Disabled Persons Act (CSDPA), which placed a duty on local authorities to investigate the level of need for services for disabled people. The Act stipulates that local authorities should undertake an initial assessment of the disabled person to determine how they could be assisted in their home life (through adaptations to their property etc) and other aspects of everyday life (washing, cooking, shopping etc).

Through the CSDPA, local authorities, for the first time, should have had robust data on disabled people in their area and a greater understanding of what services and funding they need to put in place to meet this need. While the Act initially was intended to strengthen the duties in the NAA, the CSDPA in fact created a parallel statute that augmented the NAA and this has provoked some judicial confusion as to its status (Law Commission, 2008). However, the duties of CSDPA have continued to be strengthened through the 1986 Disabled Persons (Services, Consultation and Representation) Act and the 1990 National Health Service and Community Care Act (section 46).

Similarly, the 1989 Children Act sets out the fundamental premise (the welfare principle) that in decisions involving children, the paramount consideration is the best interests of the child. This was the statutory impetus for subsequent child-centric approaches adopted in children's legislation (see, for example, the 2004 Children Act). Substantively, the Act sets out three important concepts in the welfare of children. The first is its assertion of the autonomy of the family, through the statutory definition of parental responsibility. Second, it creates a legal framework for identifying *children in need* (section 17), and sets out the duties local authorities have in relation to supporting their welfare. Finally, it puts in place duties to protect and safeguard measures for children who experience, or are likely to experience, significant harm.

The 2004 Children Act extends this child-focused nature by putting a duty on public services to ensure that *every* child has the necessary and appropriate support they need to achieve the five Every Child Matters outcomes; be healthy, stay safe, enjoy and achieve through learning, make a positive contribution to society, and achieve economic well-being (DCSF, 2008a). While the Act aimed to incorporate the principles of the UN *Convention on the Rights of the Child* (UNCRC) (UN, 1989), it has faced criticism because the five outcomes are open to wider interpretation than articles in the UNCRC.

It further puts an enforceable duty on local authorities and agencies to cooperate and collaborate in the delivery of children's services through the creation of Children's Trusts;[24] a sentiment reflected in the *National Service Framework for Children, Young People and Maternity Services* (DH, 2004b). This Act is of vital importance as it asserts for the first time the entitlement of all children to be effectively supported in order to achieve the five key life outcomes. Furthermore, it reorients the focus of all children's services towards individual outcomes for the child and, by extension, their family. Nevertheless, these improved outcomes are concerned with benefit to the individual child, rather than providing sufficient support to parents or creating sustainable and effective caring solutions that work in a whole-family context.

Continued lack of support for carers

The 1989 Children Act constructed a mutual responsibility between the state and the family for the welfare, care and support of children. Under the statutory guidance of the Act (DH, 2000), local authorities should be carrying out an initial assessment for disabled children (as classified under the criterion of *children in need*) and making provision for care. The assessment should determine whether or not the child is in need, describe their need and consider what provision can be put in place.

The state's and family's mutual responsibility from the 1989 Act was strengthened in the 1995 Carers (Recognition and Services) Act, which recognised the role of informal carers and made provision for an assessment to determine the ability of informal carers to provide care for children in need. The 2000 Carers and Disabled Children Act introduced the requirement for local authorities to inform carers of their right to receive an assessment and provides further and more nuanced support for carers. Similarly, the 2004 Carers (Equal Opportunities) Act requires further notification to parent carers of their right to an assessment. Implementation of these measures has been patchy in that assessments are not always carried out and many carers do not know they have a right to have their needs as carers met (Mencap, 2006).

The 1995 Disability Discrimination Act, as extended in 2005, states that it is unlawful to discriminate against disabled people in the provision of services, which includes services to children and their families. In the context of childcare, the 2006 Childcare Act placed new legislative duties on local authorities in England to improve well-being for young children in relation to the Every Child Matters outcomes. Furthermore, it created a new duty on local authorities to secure sufficient childcare to enable parents to work or undertake education or training leading to employment; this is called *the sufficiency duty*. However, when the national disability charity Scope undertook a national sufficiency audit of day care provision, 58% of local authorities were failing to provide inclusive provision in their area.[25] This demonstrates the lack of implementation of these policies by local authorities on the ground.

Towards personalised support

Concurrent to the development of this child-focused approach to care and support is the increasing emphasis that has been placed on personalising services.[26] In the context of purchasing, the 1989 Children Act gave local authorities the power to make direct payments (section 17a) and set up a voucher scheme for respite (short break) provision to increase the flexibility of care and support. This was strengthened through the 2001 Health and Social Care Act,[27] which gave councils a duty to offer direct payments for children's services.

A direct payment is a form of monetary payment made by councils that is devolved directly to the disabled child (or their family) who has been assessed as being eligible for certain services. The ethos behind the introduction of direct payments is to promote greater independence, choice and inclusion for disabled children and their families and ensure that they can purchase the support that the council would otherwise provide in order to meet the needs identified. The Direct Payments Guidance for England[28] highlights that it is for the council to decide the amount of direct payments an individual child receives, that it must be equivalent to the council's estimate of the reasonable cost of securing the provision of the service concerned, and that it must be sufficient to enable the disabled child's family lawfully to secure support to a standard that the council considers is reasonable to fulfil the child's needs. There is no limit on the maximum or minimum amount of direct payment either in the amount of care it is intended to purchase, or in the value of the direct payment.

Despite these legislative developments in entitlement to care and support services, implementation of these legal duties has been extremely patchy (Dobson and Middleton, 1998). This has led to families experiencing high levels of geographical variation in access to services and continuity of support (Scope, 2009). Whilst the increased personalisation of support services has been widely welcomed by the wider disability community, devolved budgets (like direct payments) have begun to produce systemic problems. The emphasis in the regulations on local discretion for councils can often lead to insufficient funding or inappropriate support for disabled children and their families (as was the case in *R (JL and LL) v Islington*[29]; see below).

The rising policy preference for devolved payments means that, practically, the balance of responsibility between the state and the parent (in the case of disabled children) is moving more towards parent control. As such, the underlying acknowledgement of mutual responsibility, as expressed in the 1989 Children Act, has shifted. The effective use of devolved budgets is reliant on the authority taking the initiative to set up timely information, advice and advocacy services or brokerage to ensure parents and children can access quality services and get the best value for money to meet their needs through a direct payment.[30] While some areas have taken advantage of the recent injection of £340 million into services, through the previous government's *Aiming High for Disabled Children* strategy (HM Treasury/DfES, 2007),[31] many families have been left without the consistent support they need (Scope, 2009). In some cases, for example, Personal Assistance (PA) support is so expensive for young disabled people on direct payments that parents have had to give up working to subsidise the care and support of their child (Scope et al, 2007).

With the increased flexibility in individual and local authority purchasing of care and support has come greater levels of inconsistency and uncertainty. The emphasis in legislation on local determination of assessment and eligibility for care and support services means that the eligibility thresholds are raised when authority budgets are under strain (CSCI, 2007). As a recent Audit Commission report (Audit Commission, 2003) illustrates:

> Families found eligibility criteria confusing, illogical and likely to change without notice. They believed that services could not explain why certain criteria applied in one service but not in another. It seemed that far from ensuring that

services were there for the people who need them, eligibility criteria and defined access routes existed in order to keep families out of contact with services and were assessed on arbitrary decisions.

Changes to eligibility

Recently, however, the vulnerability of children's care and support services to local financial pressure has been clarified in a test case that was taken as part of a wider strategic litigation approach by the Every Disabled Child Matters Campaign (EDCM). In the case of *R (JL and LL) v Islington*,[32] a local authority (Islington) reduced the number of hours of short break (respite) care that an autistic child was receiving. The discussion in the case centred on the provision in the 1989 Children Act for a general duty to provide services, but not specific steps to assess needs (section 17(1)); however, this was deemed to be in conflict with section 20, which stipulates that local authorities both *shall* and *may* provide accommodation and services for disabled children. As such, the case rested on a balancing test between the needs of the child and those of the local authority.

The judge (Mrs Justice Black) ruled that the council's eligibility criteria for disabled children's services were unlawful insofar as they made no distinction between services the authority was under a duty to provide and those that they only had a power to provide. Furthermore, the judge also found that the authority had breached its general equality duty under section 49a of the 1995 Disability Discrimination Act in failing to have due regard to the impact the new eligibility criteria would have upon disabled people with the most complex needs in the borough. Thus, the judgment held that eligibility criteria are appropriate in those situations where local authorities are using their discretionary *powers* to meet needs, but not in situations where there is an established duty to meet the need.

Lost in transition

While this judgment may provide a precedent for disabled children's eligibility for care and support services, it does not resolve the situation for disabled young people (over the age of 18) who still face strict and frequently changing eligibility thresholds for adult social care services. Adult care and support eligibility criteria are determined under Fair Access to Care Services (FACS). FACS guidance puts the risk to an individual's independence as the guiding principle in determining eligibility for care and support services (DH, 2002). Eligibility for these services is based on four levels of priority (critical, substantial, moderate and low) and councils can also take into account local resources and costs when applying and interpreting the criteria.

This ability to interpret eligibility criteria locally has inevitably led to a rationing of services; with 75% of councils now only providing care to people with *substantial* or *critical* needs, meaning many disabled people do not qualify for care and support services (LGA, 2009). The Labour government proposed changes to social care support in its Green Paper (HM Government, 2009), which could go some way towards eliminating the inconsistent application of eligibility criteria. However, the success of any new proposals hinges on the level of discretion given to local authorities.

The transition between children's and adults' care and support services continues to be fraught with difficulty and typified by anxiety and a lack of cooperation (New Philanthropy Capital, 2009). Despite the Labour government's initiatives on transition support (HM Treasury/ DfES, 2007) and legislative duties to provide services in the transition period post-education (DH, 2002), parents remain concerned about how their child's care needs will be met in the future. The inherent unreliability of children's care, described previously, and support services, together with the uncertainty of eligibility and access to appropriate care services in adulthood, leads many parents to pursue longer-term residential placements for their young disabled children. In some cases, this can lead to long stays in out-of-authority residential placements (Beresford and Cavet, 2009). Where good transition care and support is available, it can have a significant impact on the life opportunities of young disabled people (TIN et al, 2009). However, both providers and parents are increasingly concerned that the current economic climate could add to the vulnerability, uncertainty and instability of this form of support.

Section 3: Consequences of the legal tension

The cumulative tensions between the development of these different legal approaches to education and care law are highlighted by two specific policy areas that impact on the opportunities of disabled children and their families; these are parental choice (including the preference for inclusive education) and the voice of the child in decision-making.

Parental choice?

A number of the Labour government's strategies and reviews – for example, *Aiming High for Disabled Children* (HM Treasury/DfES, 2007), the Bercow Report (DCSF, 2008b), the Lamb Inquiry (DCSF, 2009a) and the Rose Review (DCSF, 2009b) – all identify that the parents of young people with SEN lack confidence in SEN services and are too often locked into confrontation with the system to get their child's needs met. This was reflected in the fact that only 59% of parents surveyed (DCSF, 2009c) through the National Indictor 54 (HM Treasury/DfES, 2007) said they had confidence in the SEN system.

Since the 1988 Education Reform Act, national policy has supported an increase in parental 'choice' (technically, the right to express a preference of school) in determining the education of their children. This has been coupled with an increase in self- or family-directed support, through devolved payments for care services. However, in the education context the strength of parental power is limited in section 316(3b) of SENDA, which sets out the situations in which parental preference can be denied and a disabled child refused a place at a mainstream school, taking into account the resources available to the authority.

For example, in the case of *Hampshire County Council v R*,[33] a child with Asperger's syndrome was transferring from primary to secondary school. The LEA had assigned a mainstream school, but his parents wanted him to attend a special school. The case went to SENDIST, who felt compelled by parental preference to name the parent's choice. The LEA appealed to the High Court who ruled that the original judgment gave too much weight to parental choice and remitted the case to a new Tribunal to carry out a balancing between the parental preference, the effect on the education of other children at the school and the resources of the authority.

More widely, case law suggests that judgments are relatively evenly balanced in terms of how often the court decides one way or another; towards the parent or the authority. While it appears that SENDIST and the courts are not solely taking the authority's word for it, neither are they allowing parental choice to be a trump card. Rather, they are adopting a balancing test in respect of choice of school, in which parental choice is only one factor to be considered, along with resources, in order to ensure that the child's needs are met.

Research, however, demonstrates that many parents of disabled children are offered no choice at all when considering a school for their child (Scope, 2002). Many parents report being offered just one option, more often than not a place at the nearest local authority special school, which caters for all disabled children regardless of their impairment type. A number of parents have had to fight to get their child accepted into their local mainstream school, and fight again to ensure their child got the support and resources they needed to fulfil their potential. Those parents whose children were offered a place at a local mainstream school frequently found that their children's needs were not adequately met by the school. This is likely to be highlighted further through the proposed new duty for Ofsted to review the progress of children with SEN and disabled children as part of school inspections. However, it will not address the systemic issue.

An extreme example of a parent having to stand up to a decision of an LEA is *MG v London Borough of Tower Hamlets*.[34] In this case, the child was not only subject to a Statement, but had also been taken into care. His mother did not accept the LEA's decision on his secondary school and appealed to SENDIST who found in favour of the mother. The LEA refused to comply with the SENDIST decision and the mother had to take the LEA to the High Court, who ordered the LEA to do as directed by the Tribunal.

Because SENDIST, and SENTW in Wales, is the most powerful legal tool available to parents to ensure their child's needs are met, we have seen attempts to fit the whole of the child's needs into an education framework. For example, the case of *TS v Chair of SENDIST and Solihull MBC*[35] focused on a parental challenge to a Statement that assigned a child with autistic spectrum disorder to a day school against the parent's request for a residential facility with a 'waking day curriculum'. The Administrative Court found against the parents and held that the fact that the child required a consistency of approach going beyond the school day did not mean either that that was necessarily an educational need or that it could only be met by way of a placement at a residential secondary school. Once again, the court has to hold the balance between the local authority's cost-saving interest and parental choice.

Audit Commission research has found that well-resourced mainstream education delivers the best outcomes for all children (Audit Commission, 2002) and gives meaningful opportunities for disabled children to be included in mainstream schools with their non-disabled peers (Ofsted, 2006). However, the tribunal system sets parents and mainstream schools up as adversaries, and Special Educational Needs Coordinators (SENCOs) are rendered unable to support parents effectively in accessing suitable provision for their disabled child. In contrast, special schools are positioned as collaborators in determining the care and curricular access their child needs and the support they require to secure legally – through the Statement – the child's admission and funding.

As such, Tribunals become centred on effective care provision in the school context, rather than the child's education itself. This is because the SEN Statement offers a stronger and relatively more accessible legal lever to simultaneous care and learning. This creates a perverse incentive for the parent to fight for specialist provision, rather than pursue inclusive options. Thus, perceived parental choice and confidence has little to do with the choice agenda, but rather is driven by the need to guarantee appropriate education and care provision for their child.

The voice of the child

Inevitably the tension that the law creates and its resulting effect on parental choice and confidence in special school education and support mean that the voice of the child can be stifled. Despite the provisions outlined in the 2004 Children Act, the 2006 Childcare Act and the 2008 Children and Young Persons Act, the child's views are still not respected in the determination of school or support preference (CRAE, 2009). This is in breach of the state's duties under the UNCRC[36] in which the recognition and status of the voice of the child is a founding principle. As the concluding observations from the UN Committee on the Rights of the Child report (2008) highlight:

> The Committee is concerned that there has been little progress to enshrine article 12 (Respect for the views of the child) in education law and policy. Furthermore, the Committee is concerned that insufficient action has been taken to ensure the rights enshrined in article 12 to children with disabilities.

Recently, however, a consultation run by the then Department for Children, Schools and Families[37] (DCSF, 2009d) on a child's own right to appeal a SEN Statement, and the Lamb Inquiry report (DCSF, 2009a) recommended that this be introduced. The proposed legislation would provide for an age limit and a competency test to be completed by the local authority or court. This legislation continues the movement towards a child-centred system, which could lead to empowerment and credibility for the young people themselves.

Nevertheless, aside from concerns around how the local authority would implement such a competency test, or whether there is sufficient support within the Tribunal system for these young people, it also may go too far in reinforcing the negative rights and entitlement system and providing direct litigious outlets for young people, further involving them, not in the development of a care plan, but in seeking remedy after the fact solely from a court of law. Ultimately, any future reform would need to ensure that it not only supports curricular access that is child-centred, but also gives equal, if not more, weight to the aspirations, preferences and concerns of the disabled child in attempting to balance the outcomes of provision for the child, the family, the authority and the wider community.

Finally, we would encourage readers to follow closely the development and emergence of children's legal rights to take appeals on their own behalf. Such provision will change disabled children's and young people's interactions with the judicial system and could bring about new challenges around the voice of the child and the weight ascribed to it in decision-making about their lives and outcomes. Currently, children's legal positioning remains invisible, but extending the right to appeal to the child could radically change this situation and case law in this area will begin to emerge as provisions giving more direct rights to the child develop.

Conclusion

Our discussion in this chapter has highlighted how the current divergence of education and care law creates inherent conflict, frustration and uncertainty for disabled children and their families. Furthermore, it places all parties in undesirable positions; with parents fighting for access to appropriate services, local authorities fighting for protection of their resources and children fighting for an equal position at the decision-making table.

As it stands, the divergent approaches taken by policy and law in these areas undermine meaningful and inclusive outcomes and opportunities for disabled children and their families. Moreover, this conflict perversely drives a preference for residential placement, which (while meeting the child's needs) excludes them from interacting with their peers, growing up with siblings and participating in family and community life. This is not ideal and the time has come to reshape the debate in light of the unintended consequences of previous well-intentioned, but less well-thought-out, policies.

We believe that in order to ensure that real parental and child choice for inclusive education can be exerted, reform of the system needs to consider how to create sustainable incentives to create inclusive educational opportunities. Furthermore, the system needs to be rebalanced to address the inherent special school bias that causes parents of disabled children to have to fight for their child's care and educational needs to be met in one provision.

This will need to involve a re-examination of the power of local authorities to act as both assessor and funder that enables the perverse incentive for them to fund cheaper segregated provision. While the Tribunal system is an important mechanism to ensure parental choice can be exerted and a child's needs can be met, it should not be so heavily relied upon to resolve the inherent tensions in the education and care frameworks. Reform needs to ensure that parents are not unnecessarily disincentivised from pursuing mainstream education options for their children by having to fight in the courts. Finally, development of a more inclusive approach needs to ensure that the individual child's wishes and opinions are heard and listened to by decision-makers, ensuring that they are given an equal place around the decision-making table.

In this, the new Coalition government has an opportunity to learn from the divergence of education and care frameworks and ensure that all children, including those with complex needs, can be educated in an inclusive educational setting. While this requires revisiting and rethinking some of their policy assumptions, it will enable them to understand how to bring about a convergence of the education and care policy and legislative frameworks to create a lasting, impactful and importantly inclusive solution to disabled children's schooling. The success of this will be, as the Prime Minister suggested in his conversation with Mr Bartley, the extent to which parents (and children) will be able to truly choose inclusive or specialist education options. The difference, we are suggesting here, is that this choice needs to be situated in a reformed system that promotes inclusive education not as an ideology, not as a principle, but rather as an embedded practice that can meet the demand that will inevitably grow from parents.

Notes

[1] Research assistance for this chapter was provided by Laura Redman.

[2] See ITN News, 'Cameron Heckled by Father of Disabled Son', 27 April 2010. Available at: http://www.youtube.com/watch?v=fivgsesKrrY&feature=fvw (accessed 31 October 2010).

[3] European Convention on Human Rights (ECHR), Article 8.

[4] ECHR, Article 2, Protocol 1.

[5] For more information, see: http://www.teachernet.gov.uk/management/resourcesfinanceandbuilding/bsf/ (accessed 31 October 2010).

[6] For more information about the activities of the Warnock Committee, see: http://nationalarchives.gov.uk/catalogue/browser.asp?CATLN=3&CATID =62186&POSCATLN=6&POSCATID=7000&j=1 (accessed 31 October 2010).

[7] For more information, see: http://www.un.org/disabilities/default. asp?id=475 (accessed 31 October 2010). The interpretative declaration reads:

> The United Kingdom Government is committed to continuing to develop an inclusive system where parents of disabled children have increasing access to mainstream schools and staff, which have the capacity to meet the needs of disabled children. The General Education System in the United Kingdom includes mainstream, and special schools, which the UK Government understands is allowed under the Convention.

[8] Repealed 1 November 1996.

[9] An appeal mechanism, first to the LEA and then to the Secretary of State, was also included in the 1981 Education Act.

[10] See, for example, *TS v Chair of SENDIST and Solihull Metropolitan Borough Council* [2009] EWHC 5.

[11] The Act also contains a legal duty for Ofsted (the education inspection body) to report on SEN.

[12] SENDIST has now become the First–tier Tribunal (Special Educational Needs and Disability) under the 2007 Tribunals, Courts and Enforcement Act. For more information, see: http://www.sendist.gov.uk/ (accessed 31 October 2010).

[13] As amended by the 2005 Disability Discrimination Act.

[14] Although the legislation fails to put a duty on schools to provide auxiliary aids and services. However, in recent case law the Court of Appeal held that after-school transport should have been provided. See *Bedfordshire County Council v Mr and Mrs Dixon-Wilkinson* [2009] EWCA Civ 678.

[15] As had previously been set in *The Universal Declaration of Human Rights* (UN, 1948), the *European Convention on Human Rights* (CoE, 1950), the *Convention on the Rights of the Child* (UN, 1989) and the 1998 Human Rights Act.

[16] As set out in the 2005 Disability Discrimination (Public Authorities) (Statutory Duties) Regulations (SI 2005/2966).

[17] See, for example, *Chavda, Fitzpatrick, and Maos v London Borough of Harrow* [2007] EWHC 3064; *R v Birmingham City Council and University of Birmingham* [2009] EWHC 688.

[18] See, for example, *R v Harlow District Council* [2009] EWHC 559.

[19] For examples of recent case law, see: *Governing Body of X School v SP and SENDIST* [2008] EWHC 389; *R (K) v SENDIST and Governing Body of Slough Grammar School* [2006] EWCA 622 (Admin); or *Governing Body of X Primary School v SENDIST, T, and National Autistic Society* [2009] EWHC 1842.

[20] [2008] UKHL 43.

[21] Following *Clark v TDG Ltd (t/a Novacold)* [1999] EWCA Civ 1091.

[22] *R (N) v Independent Appeal Panel of London Borough of Barking and Dagenham* [2009] ELR 268 (Court of Appeal) held that a child with ADHD had not been treated less favourably when she was excluded from school due to her behaviour, because a non-disabled child who behaved in the same way would have also been excluded.

[23] The 1948 National Assistance Act (Choice of Accommodation) was replaced by the 1992 National Assistance Act 1948 (Choice of Accommodation) Directions and 2001 National Assistance (Residential Accommodation) (Additional Payments and Assessment of Resources) (Amendment) (England) Regulations, and by DH (2004a) *Local Authority Circular 20: Guidance on National Assistance Act 1948 (Choice of Accommodation) Directions 1992 and National Assistance (Residential Accommodation) (Additional Payments and Assessment of Resources) (Amendment) (England) Regulations 2001.*

[24] At the time of writing, the government was currently consulting on New Statutory Children's Trust Guidance and New Children and Young People's Plan Regulations.

[25] Personal correspondence with Scope.

[26] Following the direction set out in relation to adult social care in *Putting People First: A Shared Vision and Commitment to the Transformation of Adult Social Care* (HM Government, 2007).

[27] This further amends the 1996 Community Care (Direct Payments) Act.

[28] DH (2003b) *Community Care, Services for Carers and Children's Services (Direct Payments) Guidance (England)*, superseded by DH (2009) *Guidance on Direct Payments: For Community Care, Services for Carers and Children's Services.*

[29] [2009] EWHC 458 (Admin).

[30] As expressed in the 1989 Children Act and the *Direct Payments Guidance for England* (DH, 2003a).

[31] For example, see Suffolk's Activities Unlimited brokerage: www.activities-unlimited.co.uk/ (accessed 31 October 2010).

[32] *R (JL and LL) v Islington LBC* [2009] EWHC 458 (Admin).

[33] [2009] EWHC 626 (Admin).

[34] *R (MG) v London Borough of Tower Hamlets* [2008] EWHC 1577 (Admin).

[35] *R (TS) v Bowen (Chair of SENDIST) & Solihull Metropolitan Borough Council* [2009] EWHC 5 (Admin).

[36] Also expressed in Article 23 of the UN *Convention on the Rights of Persons with Disabilities* (UN, 2006), which acknowledges disabled children as a distinctive group of children who face particular disadvantage. Available at: www.un.org/disabilities/documents/convention/convoptprot-e.pdf

[37] Now the Department for Education.

References

Audit Commission (2002) *Special Educational Needs: A Mainstream Issue*, London: Audit Commission.

Audit Commission (2003) *Services for Disabled Children: A Review of Services for Disabled Children and Their Families*, London: Audit Commission.

Beresford, B. and Cavet, J. (2009) *Transitions to Adult Services by Disabled Young People Leaving Out of Authority Residential Schools*, York: Social Policy Research Unit.

Conservative Party (2010) *Invitation to Join the Government of Britain (Manifesto)*, London: Conservative Party.

Council of Europe (1950) *Convention for the Protection of Human Rights and Fundamental Freedoms*, Rome: Council of Europe.

CRAE (Children's Rights Alliance England) (2009) *State of Children's Rights in England 2009*, London: CRAE.

CSCI (Commission for Social Care Inspection) (2007) *Children's Services: CSCI Findings, 2004–07*, London: CSCI.

DCSF (Department for Children, Schools and Families) (2008a) *Every Child Matters Outcomes Framework*, London: DCSF.

DCSF (2008b) *The Bercow Report: A Review of Services for Children and Young People (0–19) with Speech, Language and Communication Needs*, London: DCSF.

DCSF (2009a) *Lamb Inquiry: Special Educational Needs and Parental Confidence*, London: DCSF.

DCSF (2009b) *Independent [Rose] Review of the Primary Curriculum: Final Report*, London: DCSF.

DCSF (2009c) *Parental Experience of Services for Disabled Children*, London: DCSF.

Department for Education (2011) *Support and Aspiration: A New Approach to Special Educational Needs and Disability: A Consultation,* Norwich: TSO.

DfES (Department for Education and Skills) (2001) *Special Educational Needs: Code of Practice,* London: DfES.

DfES (2004) *Removing Barriers to Achievement: The Government's Strategy for Special Educational Needs,* London: DfES.

DH (Department of Health) (2000) *Framework for the Assessment of Children in Need and their Families,* London: DH.

DH (2002) *Local Authority Circular 13: Fair Access to Care Services: Guidance on Eligibility Criteria for Adult Social Care,* London: DH

DH (2003a) *Direct Payments Guidance for England,* London: DH.

DH (2003b) *Community Care, Services for Carers and Children's Services (Direct Payments) Guidance (England),* London: DH.

DH (2004a) *Local Authority Circular 20: Guidance on National Assistance Act 1948 (Choice of Accommodation) Directions 1992 and National Assistance (Residential Accommodation) (Additional Payments and Assessment of Resources) (Amendment) (England) Regulations 2001,* London: DH.

DH (2004b) *National Service Framework for Children, Young People and Maternity Services,* London: DH.

DH (2009) *Guidance on Direct Payments: For Community Care, Services for Carers and Children's Services,* London: DH.

Dobson, B. and Middleton, S. (1998) *Paying to Care: The Cost of Childhood Disability,* York: Joseph Rowntree Foundation.

Emerson, E. (2009) *Estimating Future Numbers of Adults with Profound Multiple Learning Disabilities in England,* London: DH.

HM Government (1978) *Report of the Committee of Enquiry into the Education of Handicapped Children and Young People* (The Warnock Report), London: HM Government.

HM Government (2007) *Putting People First: A Shared Vision and Commitment to the Transformation of Adult Social Care,* London: HM Government.

HM Government (2009) *Shaping the Future of Care Together,* London: HM Government.

HM Government (2010) *The Coalition: Our Programme for Government,* London: HM Government.

HM Treasury/DfES (2007) *Aiming High for Disabled Children (AHDC): Better Support for Families,* London: HM Government.

IPPR (Institute for Public Policy Research) (2007) *Disability 2020: Opportunities for the Full and Equal Citizenship of Disabled People in Britain in 2020,* London: IPPR.

Law Commission (2008) *Adult Social Care: Scoping Report*, London: Law Commission.

Local Government Association (2009) *Facing Facts and Tomorrow's Reality Today, the Extra Costs of Care*, London: LGA.

Mencap (2006) *Breaking Point: Families Still Need a Break*, London: Mencap.

New Philanthropy Capital (2009) *Rights of Passage: Supporting Disabled Young People through the Transition to Adulthood*, London: NPC.

Ofsted (2006) *Inclusion: Does It Matter Where Pupils Are Taught?*, London: Ofsted.

PricewaterhouseCoopers (2006) *Market for Disabled Children's Services: A Review*, London: PwC.

Scope (2002) *The Direct Approach: Disabled People's Experiences of Direct Payments*, London: Scope.

Scope (2009) *Disabled Families in Flux: Removing Barriers to Family Life*, London: Scope.

Scope, Treehouse and Working Families (2007) *Making Work Work for Parents of Disabled Children: Achieving a Work/Life Balance with a Disabled Child*, London: Scope.

Transition Information Network (2009) *TransMap: From Theory into Practice (the Underlying Principles in Supporting Disabled Young People in Transition to Adulthood)*, London: TIN.

UN (United Nations) (1948) *The Universal Declaration of Human Rights*, Geneva: UN.

UN (1989) *Convention on the Rights of the Child,* Geneva: UN.

UN (2006) *Convention on the Rights of Persons with Disabilities,* Geneva: UN.

UNESCO (United Nations Educational, Scientific and Cultural Organization) (1994) *The Salamanca Statement and Framework for Action on Special Needs Education*, Geneva, UNESCO.

THREE

From SEN to Sen: could the 'capabilities' approach transform the educational opportunities of disabled children?

Neil Crowther

Introduction

The philosophy of inclusive education is based upon recognition of education as an inalienable human right. Yet the UK falls considerably short of delivering this right in practice to disabled children and children with learning difficulties.

Despite progress, in 2010 disabled children continued to face profound inequalities in relation to their access to, participation in and outcomes from our education system. The costs of this disadvantage to the individuals concerned, their families and to society as a whole are enormous.

In the 30 years since the Warnock Report initiated the drive towards inclusive education, a succession of Acts of Parliament and policy initiatives have sought to address the opportunities of disabled children and children with learning difficulties. Divorced from the pursuit of equality, however, this framework continues to fail to recognise and systematically address the structural causes of inequality and disadvantage both within and outside our education system. In this sense, the present special educational needs (SEN) system might be viewed as an extremely expensive and often futile effort to ameliorate the effects of this failure. Such a view appears to be supported by Ofsted, which in its *Special Educational Needs and Disability Review* (2010) concluded that 'as many as half of all pupils identified for SEN School Action would not be identified as having special educational needs if schools focused on improving teaching and learning for all, with individual goals for improvement'.

Our approach to the education of disabled children has failed to keep step with wider developments concerning disability rights. In the fields of employment and public services, real efforts are being made to reconcile social and economic welfare with civil and political rights, with increasing emphasis on removing barriers, promoting individual autonomy and supporting full participation. Yet in relation to the most formative years of disabled people's lives, at school, we remain doggedly stuck to an outmoded social welfare model – meeting 'special needs', which are considered to be born out of individual 'deficits'. In the meantime, the philosophy of inclusion has become a tarnished and contested 'political football', which has arguably reached the limits of its usefulness as a political and practical force for change.

In this chapter, I will argue that the capabilities approach, most famously advanced by the Nobel Laureate economist Amartya Sen, offers a fruitful political and practical way forward in making the human right to education a practical reality.

Ratify now![1]

On 8 July 2009, a UK government official 'deposited the instrument of ratification' at the United Nations' headquarters in New York, expressing the United Kingdom's consent to be legally bound by the UN Convention on the Rights of Persons with Disabilities (UNCRPD).[2]

This historic milestone in disabled people's struggle for human rights should have been a major cause for celebration. The UK government and activists enjoyed an influential role in negotiating what is the first international human rights treaty of the 21st century, playing to Britain's strength as a world leader on disability rights. Unfortunately, to the dismay of many disability organisations, upon ratification the government elected to express a series of reservations, including both a reservation and an interpretative declaration on Article 24 of the Convention concerning education. These have the effect of withholding or limiting the extent to which the government gives its consent to be bound by the Convention in these areas.

In relation to education, while the government helpfully clarified that it 'is committed to continuing to develop an inclusive system where parents of disabled children have increasing access to mainstream schools and staff, which have the capacity to meet the needs of disabled children' it entered a declaration stating that 'The General Education System in the United Kingdom includes mainstream, and special schools, which the UK Government understands is allowed under the Convention' (DWP, 2009).

Reflecting the fact that a number of disabled children attend special schools, including residential special schools, away from the communities in which their families live, the government also entered a reservation stating that 'The United Kingdom reserves the right for disabled children to be educated outside their local community where more appropriate education provision is available elsewhere. Nevertheless, parents of disabled children have the same opportunity as other parents to state a preference for the school at which they wish their child to be educated'.[3]

On the one hand, it could be argued that the declaration and reservation display a degree of honesty concerning the current incapacity of the UK education system to meet the Convention's requirement that 'Persons with disabilities can access an inclusive, quality and free primary education and secondary education on an equal basis with others in the communities in which they live'. After all, it is inconceivable that a number of countries which have ratified without reservations are better positioned than the UK to deliver this right in practice. States are empowered to withdraw or modify them in future if they believe them to be no longer necessary.

Unfortunately, however, despite the clarification, neither the wording of the reservation nor the declaration indicated positions that were 'time-limited' and merely reflected the current 'state of play'. Furthermore, as it is generally held that Article 24 does not confer justiciable civil and political rights, but social and economic rights designed to be 'progressively realised' over time, a declaration or reservation would not be necessary to achieve such a purpose. Rather the wording could be understood to indicate that the previous government would have maintained this position, irrespective of the progress made on improving access to mainstream schools, as a matter of principle. Despite its commitment to widen access to mainstream education over time, the reservation and declaration therefore appear to confirm what many had suspected – that the previous government had resiled from its past commitment to inclusion.

A very inclusive notion of inclusion

The true meaning of 'inclusion' has of course always been disputed and devoid of consensus, and has often been reduced to an unhelpful, misleading and sterile debate focused solely on *where* disabled children are educated rather than the quality of education and its outcomes.

Some oppose the concept altogether, believing special schools to play an important and legitimate role in ensuring disabled children have access to the specialist education and support they require. In its 2010 general election manifesto, the Conservative Party pledged to 'call a moratorium on the ideologically-driven closure of special schools and end the bias towards the inclusion of children with special needs in mainstream schools' (Conservative Party, 2010).

Some disability activists have made 'non-segregation' their primary goal, arguing that segregation violates children's human rights to non-discrimination and have sought as a matter of public policy the active closure of special schools by a specified date.[4] Others take a more pragmatic approach, ultimately preferring inclusion, but recognising that in some cases mainstream schools are at present lacking in the capacity required to provide an effective education to some children, and therefore viewing the continuation of special schools as a necessary 'stopgap'. They advocate a gradualist approach including 'co-locating' specialist units within mainstream schools, the sharing of resources and expertise between mainstream and special schools to build capacity and expertise, or children spending some time in both special and mainstream education to ensure that their specialist support needs are met. The last government, at some point over the last decade and in an apparent attempt to encompass all of the above positions, took the curious step of ceasing to refer to inclusive schools and instead to an 'inclusive education system' in which the full range of school provision – special, mainstream and everything in-between – enjoyed a valid and ongoing role.

It is this position, and the legal framework underpinning it, which is reflected in the reservation and declaration concerning the Convention. If inclusion can mean all of the above, then arguably it means nothing at all and has lost its practical use as a force for change.

In recent years, 'inclusion' as it was originally understood does appear to have diminished in influence and is being overwhelmed by other imperatives. Despite the fact that the number of 'specialist' places for children with SEN has remained broadly static, the closure of special schools – and, therefore, by association, inclusion – is seen by significant players to undermine the political shibboleth of promoting parental choice. The policy of inclusion is held responsible for the impact of the declining ability of teachers to address behaviour and discipline in the classroom – the issue consistently making an appearance in the motions of annual teaching union conferences. Practice has failed to keep pace with the changing profile of disabled children, and in particular what is either an increase in or increased recognition of what have been called 'neuro-diverse profiles' including autism, attention deficit disorders and dyspraxia, as well as a growth in the number of children considered to have what are termed 'complex needs'. This has caused some to question whether there are disabled children whose impairments make them de facto uneducable in mainstream settings.

Moreover, although the numbers of disabled children attending mainstream schools have steadily increased since the policy of inclusion began to be implemented in the early 1980s, and the rates of educational attainment by disabled children have improved, disabled children and young people, including those with SEN, continue to face deep and persistent disadvantage. Research for the Disability Debate found that in England in 2007/08, nearly 74% of those without SEN achieved five or more GCSEs at grades A★ to C, compared with around 30% of those with SEN but without a Statement and 11% of those with SEN and with a Statement. At age 19, 27% of disabled young people were not in any form of employment, education or training (NEET), compared with 9% of their non-disabled peers. Disabled young people aged 16–24 were twice as likely as their non-disabled peers to have no qualifications at all, and many reported far lower expectations and aspirations. Around half of all disabled people of working age were not in paid employment, increasing to over 80% of adults with learning disabilities. Children with SEN were eight times more likely to be excluded from school. Six out of 10 children referred to Youth Offending Teams had been identified as having SEN. The Prison Reform Trust estimated that between 20% and 30% of the prison population had a learning disability or difficulty.

The resulting social and economic costs are vast, yet the idea that this is a product of systemic failure remains obscured by the individual deficit model that dominates thinking around disabled children and others who face challenges in their early lives.

The dominance of 'special educational needs'

The 1996 Education Act, augmented by the 2001 Special Educational Needs and Disability Act (SENDA), presumes that a child identified as having SEN should be educated in a mainstream school unless it is against the wishes of their parents or in conflict with the effective education of other children. The primary – and important – 'right' available in education law to the parents of disabled children is to an assessment of SEN and that such assessed needs must be met.

Although the 1995 Disability Discrimination Act (DDA) was extended to place duties on schools via SENDA, it was done so in a very limited way in contrast with DDA duties on employers or service providers, with little practical or cultural impact. Unlike employers and service providers, schools were not placed under duties to make reasonable adjustments in respect of 'auxiliary aids and services' or physical access. The former would continue to be the province of the SEN framework, and the latter was pursued via a non-justiciable 'planning duty' upon schools. In effect, the SEN framework and DDA 'coexisted' rather than the DDA signalling a new rights-based approach to which the SEN framework would be subordinated. The 2005 Disability Discrimination Act placed schools, in line with the rest of the public sector, under a new duty to promote equality of opportunity for disabled people. However, evidence suggests few schools have met their duty as evidenced by the production and implementation of a disability equality scheme (DCSF, 2008b).

In the intervening years, it has become clear that the supposed 'jigsaw' of the SEN and DDA fails to attend to the full picture, and that the framework is failing to deliver. In its *Special Educational Needs and Disability Review*, Ofsted (2010) found that:

> When a child was identified as having special educational needs at School Action Plus, or especially with a statement, this usually led to the allocation of further additional resources from within and outside the school. However, inspectors found that this additional provision was often not of good quality and did not lead to significantly better outcomes for the child or young person. For pupils identified for support at School Action level, the additional provision was often making up for poor whole-class teaching or pastoral support. Even for pupils at School Action Plus level and with statements, the provision was often not meeting their needs effectively, either because it was not appropriate or not of good quality or both.

The report goes on to say that too often the various public agencies involved in meeting SEN 'focused simply on whether a service was or was not being provided rather than whether it was effective'.

This is not simply a matter of how the SEN system is or is not implemented. It is born of the fact that, unlike disability rights law, the principal objective of the SEN framework is not to promote the 'full participation' of disabled children, but the more limited objective of mitigating 'learning difficulties', which too often continue to be seen as intrinsic to the child rather than barriers for the system to overcome. The philosophy of 'meeting 'needs' is fundamentally different from that of pursuing more equitable outcomes through whole-system change to address barriers or through providing personalised learning and support.

There are children with rights under the DDA who require resources and support but who are not considered to have SEN, such as children with particular medical needs relating to conditions such as diabetes or cancer. Furthermore, some children identified as having SEN do not meet the definition of disability in the DDA. As discussed earlier, the SEN framework addresses learning difficulties, not barriers to full participation. This means, for example, that while a child with SEN may gain access to a teaching assistant in the classroom – to mitigate 'learning difficulties' – they may not have the support of a personal assistant in the playground, or the opportunity to take part in extra-curricular activities, both of which may be critical to establishing friendships and their longer-term development in keeping with their rights as children. The picture is complicated further by the employment of the concept of 'vulnerability' by the wider children's policy framework to identify and prioritise needs.

SEN – an almost 30-year-old bureaucratic framework for the identification of needs and allocation of resources to children identified as having 'learning difficulties' – continues to provide the definitive understanding of and approach to the education of disabled children. The DDA has barely made a dent in its dominance. Arguably, the reservation and declaration expressed by the previous UK government concerning Article 24 of the UNCRPD represents a tacit admission that, despite annual public expenditure of several billion pounds on meeting SEN, the education system continues to fail hundreds of thousands of children every year at huge cost to both their lives and the wider public.

Of course, the British education system is not alone in having failed to reconcile the delivery of social and economic, often compensatory, 'welfare' with promoting the civil and political rights of its subjects. The defining struggle of the disabled people's independent living movement in Britain and elsewhere has been to seek to overcome such paternalism through advocating legislative and public service reform, centred on rights to self-determination and support for full participation. This goal was captured in the mission statement of the Disability Rights Commission, which worked towards 'a society in which all disabled people can participate fully as equal citizens'. In recent years this struggle found some common cause with reformers promoting a transformation from a 'passive' to an 'active' welfare state, most notably though the adoption of 'independent living' (or a version of it) as official government policy and through the widespread acceptance of the social, rather than medical, model of disability (Prime Minister's Strategy Unit, 2005). However, while the objectives of promoting choice, control and participation are increasingly reshaping welfare policy and public services such as health, social care and employment support, these principles have had little impact on our approach to disabled children, or their education. This clearly contributes to the disadvantage these children face throughout their lives and undermines the effectiveness of policies to promote independent living and economic participation in adulthood.

Given the government's resistance to ratifying the UNCRPD in full, it may, then, seem counter-intuitive to propose that a human rights-based approach is the way to build a new consensus. However, I hope to demonstrate that such an approach – by making the focus of this debate the promotion of individual dignity and optimising potential – would help us get past the often unhelpful distractions that have characterised the stale and polarised debate on inclusion and to create a new debate about the achievement of goals that all are likely to share.

Towards a human rights-based approach to disabled children and education

Education has been formally recognised as a human right since the adoption of the Universal Declaration on Human Rights in 1948. A succession of international treaties have affirmed and developed this right since, including the UNCRPD and the United Nations Convention on the Rights of the Child (UNCRC).[5]

In its publication *A Human Rights Based Approach to Education for All*, UNICEF (2007) articulates a straightforward goal of a human rights-based approach to education: 'to assure every child a quality education that respects and promotes her or his right to dignity and optimum development'.

The report goes on to offer a three-part conceptual framework for a human rights-based approach to education, based upon the UNCRC:

1. The right of access to education
   * Education throughout all stages of childhood and beyond.
   * Availability and accessibility of education.
   * Equality of opportunity.
2. The right to quality education
   * A broad, relevant and inclusive curriculum.
   * Rights-based learning and assessment.
   * Child-friendly, safe and healthy environments.

3. The right to respect in the learning environment
   - Respect for identity.
   - Respect for participation rights.
   - Respect for integrity.

The UNCRC is not confined to imposing limits only on the state, but also on parents. The best interests of the child must be a primary consideration in all matters affecting them, their views must be given serious consideration and the child's evolving capacities must be respected. Parental rights to choose their children's education are not absolute and are seen to decline as children grow older. In the case of conflict between parental choice and the best interests of the child, the child should always be the priority.

The UNCRPD has latterly spelt out the steps that need to be taken to make such rights a practical reality for disabled children:

a) persons with disabilities are not excluded from the general education system on the basis of disability, and that children with disabilities are not excluded from free and compulsory primary education, or from secondary education, on the basis of disability;
b) persons with disabilities can access an inclusive, quality and free primary education and secondary education on an equal basis with others in the communities in which they live;
c) reasonable accommodation of the individual's requirements is provided;
d) persons with disabilities receive the support required, within the general education system, to facilitate their effective education; and
e) effective individualised support measures are provided in environments that maximise academic and social development, consistent with the goal of full inclusion.

This high-level framework is helpful in reframing the debate about disabled children's education, but implementing a human rights-based approach on the ground requires something more.

From SEN to Sen – employing a 'capabilities' approach' to promote the human rights of disabled children

The phrase 'capabilities' generally causes alarm bells to start ringing among disability rights activists, associated as it is with medical or functional assessments underpinning social security entitlements.

However, if we are able to get past this unhelpful phrase, further exploration shows that in fact the approach, most famously articulated by the Nobel Laureate economist Amartya Sen and developed by among others Martha Nussbaum, has much in common with the most influential ideas of the disability movement, namely the social model of disability and independent living, as well as ideas familiar to educationalists such as 'person-centred learning'.

Sen's thinking was developed in the context of welfare economics, where it went on to inspire the creation of the United Nations Human Development Index. A capabilities approach is an approach to human rights and equality that focuses not simply on people's *freedom from* harm, undue interference or discrimination, but also on what is required to accord them the *freedom to* flourish as human beings, ensuring they have genuine autonomy to shape a life worth living. 'Capabilities' are in fact the 'substantive freedoms' that enable people to achieve what Sen refers to as 'functionings' – such as the ability to stay safe, to maintain good health, to have a voice in decisions affecting our lives, to acquire knowledge, to interact with others, or to play – which can either confirm or deny us the opportunity to be and do things that are of value to us in our lives and to develop as human beings. Using a capabilities approach, the measure of equality is 'what people are actually able to be and do' (Nussbaum, 2000). Sen calls inequalities in the achievement of these freedoms 'capability deprivation'.

Critically, the capabilities approach maintains commitment to the universality and indivisibility of human rights, but it expressly recognises that people are not equally placed to realise them in practice and, therefore, require different resources and interventions to do so. Sen claims that 'human diversity is no secondary consideration (to be ignored or to be introduced "later on"); it is a fundamental of our interest in equality'. He argues that human beings are diverse in three fundamental ways: in our personal characteristics, such as gender, age or impairment; in our external circumstances, such as inherited wealth and assets, and environmental factors, such as social and cultural arrangements; and, critically, in our ability to convert resources into desired 'functionings'.

If we reconceptualise disability within the capabilities approach, then disability can be understood as an aspect of human diversity that causes a restriction in the set of functionings available to the person concerned, and by consequence as 'capability deprivation'.

Terzi (2008) argues that:

rethinking disability in terms of capabilities implies considering what the full set of capabilities one person can choose from are and evaluating the impact of impairment on this set of freedoms. It implies, moreover, considering the interface between the individual and the environmental characteristics in assessing what circumstantial elements may lead to an impairment becoming disability, and how this impacts capabilities.

Terzi goes on to argue that a capabilities approach:

> provides a framework that allows the interplay between the theoretical dimension of conceptualising disability and special educational needs as aspects of human diversity (the difference) and the political level of responding to the equal entitlement of all children to education (the sameness).

Using this approach, our measure of success ceases to be whether we are meeting 'special educational needs', but whether we are addressing the 'capability deprivations' faced by all children, including children with impairments, both in accessing their rights as children and in terms of the role education plays in equipping children with the capabilities to get on in life.

Like the concept of 'independent living', which has heralded reforms such as self-directed support and individual budgets, the capabilities approach requires steps to overcome the damaging impact of fragmented public services through 'person-centred' planning and delivery – or consumption – of services. Indivisible human rights cannot be delivered by divisive public services. Furthermore, such an approach suggests a shift in power and responsibilities from the professionals involved in the provision and delivery of services to the individuals requiring them. This has the effect of transforming disabled individuals from 'objects' of public services to 'co-producers', with professionals increasingly relinquishing control and assuming the role of partners, navigators and facilitators in supporting people (in this case disabled children and their parents) to pursue their life goals within a more genuine participatory democracy. Educationalists will perhaps be more familiar with the language of 'person-centred learning', which implies many of the same disciplines and approaches.

Of course, the capabilities approach is not without its critics. Some have questioned how far the approach can be made operational. Sen has been criticised for not himself identifying valuable capabilities. Others have argued that Sen goes too far in insisting that certain capabilities are de facto valuable, suggesting that there is too much disagreement between people to do this. In practice, the determination of valuable capabilities – and by definition the obligations of a society to secure them for its citizens – should rely upon democratic deliberation where they concern matters over and above the meeting of fundamental human rights. In England, the 'Every Child Matters' (DCSF, 2008a) framework focuses upon what are in effect five core 'capabilities': to be healthy, stay safe, enjoy and achieve through learning, make a positive contribution to society, and achieve economic well-being. It has been argued that the capabilities approach does not provide a useful framework through which to make interpersonal comparisons of well-being given the potential of arguments over the relative weights to be assigned to different capabilities. Sen, however, argues that there is a large degree of consensus between people in the way they rank the importance of different capabilities, and again the five goals of Every Child Matters are instructive and provide a means for comparison in the performance of different children. Finally, the information requirements of the capabilities approach are extremely high and could be deemed burdensome by those required to collate data. At a time of public spending cuts, this is a significant problem. However, it is worth noting that public authorities, including schools, already collate a significant amount of data concerning the progress of all children, which could be used much more efficiently than at present if allied to the task of addressing capability deprivations.

Turning theory into practice – implementing a capabilities approach

A capabilities approach has the potential to provide a human rights-based framework through which to address many of the shortfalls in and criticisms of our existing approach to the education of disabled children and children with SEN. Critically, a capabilities approach would herald a shift in priorities concerning the primary success measure of our school system. Its focus would be a deeper and wider conception of human development than that indicated solely by educational attainment, broadly in keeping with the aspirations of the Every Child Matters framework. In doing so, the distance travelled by children in the achievement of particular 'functionings' would be as important a measure as examinations passed in recognising the achievement of children, in measuring not only school success, but also the broader framework of children's policy and services, and in terms of identifying inequalities and their causes.

Mindful of the adage 'what gets measured gets done', it will be important to amend the indicators against which the school system is measured and the focus of school and wider children's services inspections. The Equality and Human Rights Commission (EHRC), in partnership with the Government Equality Office and in consultation with a wide range of stakeholders including government departments, has developed an 'equality measurement framework'. The framework draws on the capabilities approach.

Such legal and policy frameworks as do exist, such as the Disability Discrimination Act, the SEN framework in England and Wales, the Additional Support for Learning framework in Scotland, and the 2004 Children Act, would collectively be subordinated to the protection and promotion of capabilities. This enables us more clearly to recognise gaps or deficiencies in the way these systems are focused or in their coverage and to introduce more cohesive reform.

The 2010 Equality Act will hopefully address one such deficiency when it is implemented. After many years of resistance, the previous government agreed to extend to schools the duty to provide – as a reasonable adjustment – auxiliary aids and services. This amendment is primarily important in addressing the practical matter of ensuring that children without statements of SEN or who require such adjustments but are not identified as having SEN, such as children with insulin-dependent diabetes, have a right to access them. However, it potentially has a much more far-reaching significance, rendering the SEN framework subordinate to the pursuit of disability rights. The new clause allows us to reposition the SEN framework – insofar as it continues to exist – as part of the framework for securing the adjustments some children require to overcome discrimination. As such, its express purpose becomes that of addressing particular 'capability deprivations' in a similar way to the role of access to work or disabled students allowance, both of which provide access to resources to facilitate participation in employment or higher education respectively.

Despite the five Every Child Matters outcomes, the various statutory frameworks concerning disabled children are based on different philosophies, objectives and definitions creating significant problems and arguably undermining the benefits of the 'duty to cooperate' placed upon various public services in the 2004 Children Act. It is complicated enough for public bodies to align their priorities and work-plans, let alone when they lack a single unified purpose and collective sense of impact and achievement. Furthermore, it is extremely confusing for parents to be forced to pursue their children's rights via multiple and wildly different legislative frameworks. A rights-based approach would provide clarity both for service providers and parents alike, as well as providing – through the concept of capability deprivation – a common approach to prioritising and targeted increasingly scarce resources in a fair way.

In the meantime, individual budgets provide one way through which the effects of such disunity can be mitigated, and via which both parents and children can assume a greater role both in determining goals and how best they can be met, drawing together children's health and social services and resources and support accessed via the SEN framework.

Related to this, greater attention must be paid in law, policy and practice to the 'best interests' principle that underpins the UNCRC. In promoting the voice of disabled children, children in England and Wales over the age of 12 should enjoy the same rights as their counterparts in Scotland to bring cases of discrimination in their own name. Some children should have access to independent advocacy – in particular children with learning disabilities, communication impairments or 'looked-after' children – to facilitate their being able to exercise choice and control in matters affecting them.

At present, the 'best interests' principle is normally assumed to be a right available to the parents of children with SEN to elect to send their child to a special school. It is unclear to what degree local education authorities and tribunals interpret the 'best interests' principle of the UNCRC as a constraint on parental choice where there is good reason to believe placement in a special school would not be in a child's best interests.

A human rights-based approach is not only concerned with access to education, but equally is about promoting a culture of respect for human rights through ethos, culture and curriculum. The EHRC's Human Rights Inquiry cited Knights Enham Primary School in Hampshire as an example of the difference a human rights-based approach can make. Knights Enham's catchment area is a poor part of Hampshire: the area is in the bottom 6% of deprivation indices in the UK, and 40% of children are on free school meals. Since the school adopted the rights-based approach in 2003, unauthorised absence has dropped, exclusions are down from eight children in 2002/03 to only one in 2007/08, and SATS scores have risen from 133 to 252. Head teacher Anne Hughes describes the change since adopting a human rights-based approach as 'remarkable'. The school began by implementing the approach in one of the school's two Year 6 classes. They found that "very quickly we started to notice differences in behaviour and attitude between the two classes. The children who were taught about human rights were more tolerant of one another, they listened to each other, and they were more interested in global issues". Reflecting the principle of co-production, staff, parents and children sign up to a 'Home–School Agreement', which states their rights and responsibilities. At the beginning of each year, all the classes produce a charter outlining the rights the children want and the responsibilities that go with them. William Cooper, a pupil at the school, is quoted as saying "We've all got to respect people's rights, so we set an example for the younger kids", while another, Megan Glendon, said "If we want the right to express ourselves, that means we have the responsibility to listen when other people talk".[6]

On the question of *where* disabled children should be educated, it is clear that to have no choice but to be educated separately from one's peers on the basis of disability is a capability deprivation. However, it is also clear that attendance at some mainstream schools would currently compound rather than alleviate other capability deprivations faced by some disabled children as they lack the ethos, resources, skills or access to wider public service support necessary to address them. As such, the holistic nature of the capabilities approach would provide that alternative modes of education were justified in particular cases where it is in the best interests of a particular child. However, it would demand a wider programme of 'progressive realisation' of the full range of capabilities over time.

Inclusion is dead, long live inclusion

'Inclusion' has sadly become a tarnished brand in Britain. A contested idea, it is now too often reduced to a political football in the battle over which political party does most to promote parental choice. However, the human rights principles underpinning it – that all children are to be considered equal in dignity and worth, have a right to education and that education systems must be founded upon respect for and accommodation of diversity – endure. The capabilities approach provides a potential way forward in making these rights a reality.

In the words of Robert Prouty (quoted in UNICEF, 2007):

> My right to learn
> I do not have to earn
> The right to learn.
> It's mine.

And if because
Of faulty laws
And errors of design,
And far too many places where
Still far too many people do not care –
If because of all these things, and more,
For me, the classroom door,
With someone who can teach,
Is still beyond my reach,
Still out of sight,
Those wrongs do not remove my right.

So here I am. I too
Am one of you
And by God's grace,
And yours, I'll find my place.

We haven't met.
You do not know me yet
And so
You don't yet know
That there is much that I can give you in return.
The future is my name
And all I claim
Is this: my right to learn.

Notes

1 See: http://ratifynow.org/

2 See: www.un.org/disabilities/default.asp?navid=13&pid=150

3 Quotations from the Explanatory Memorandum, see www.equalityhumanrights.com/human-rights/international-framework/human-rights-submissions/rights-of-disabled-people/governments-explanatory-memorandum-and-commission-response/

4 See, for example, the Alliance for Inclusive Education 2020 campaign, www.csie.org.uk/news/press-releases/2020-mar05.pdf

5 For the full text of the UN Convention on the Rights of the Child, see www2.ohchr.org/english/law/crc.htm

6 For further information, see: www.equalityhumanrights.com/human-rights/human-rights-inquiry/case-studies/knights-enham-primary-school-hampshire/

References

Conservative Party (2010) *Mending Our Broken Society*, London: Conservative Party.

DCSF (Department for Children, Schools and Families) (2008a) *Every Child Matters Outcomes Framework*, London: DCSF.

DSCF (2008b) *Secretary of State Report on Progress towards Disability Equality across the Children's and Education Sector,* www.dcsf.gov.uk/des/sosreport.shtml

Disability Rights Commission (2008) *The Disability Agenda*, London: Disability Rights Commission.

DWP (Department for Work and Pensions) (2009) *Explanatory Memorandum on the United Nations Convention on the Rights of Persons with Disabilities laid before the UK Parliament*, London: DWP.

Nussbaum, M.C. (2000) *Women and Human Development: The Capabilities Approach*, Cambridge: Cambridge University Press.

Ofsted (2010) *Special Educational Needs and Disability Review*, London: Ofsted

Prime Minister's Strategy Unit (2005) *Improving the Life Chances of Disabled People*, London: Prime Minister's Strategy Unit/Cabinet Office.

Terzi, L. (2008) 'Beyond the Dilemma of Difference: The Capability Approach to Disability and Special Educational Needs', in M. McLaughlin and L. Florian (eds) *Disability Classification in Education: Issues and Perspectives,* Thousand Oaks, CA: Corwin Press.

UNICEF (2007) *A Human Rights-Based Approach to Education for All,* New York, Paris: UNICEF, UNESCO.

FOUR

Multi-agency working and disabled children and young people: from 'what works' to 'active becoming'

Liz Todd

Introduction

This chapter considers the assumptions and implications of policy developments in multi-agency working over at least the last 30 years for the support of disabled children and young people. I look at three policy strands: post-Warnock statutory special educational needs (SEN) assessment; inclusive education; and the Every Child Matters agenda. My focus is on education, and although the actual policies referred to would vary in other contexts, the overall argument will, I claim, apply to all. There has been a constantly renewed call to improve multi-agency working and, more recently, for far-reaching structural changes to integrate services. However, it is questionable as to whether this has been for the benefit of disabled children and young people. I make the case that problems in multi-agency working have been repeatedly conceptualised in ways that do not tell the whole story and, therefore, do not make it easy for improvements to happen.

Multi-agency working has been understood in terms of 'what works', looking at systems and communication, rather than in terms of the complex politics around the professional role and relationships. The perspectives of parents and young people on how services should work with them have been ignored or ineffectively included. In this chapter, misconceptions of multi-agency working are traced through some key policy developments leading to different kinds of thinking that might take us in other directions. I propose an understanding not of multi-agency working per se, but rather one that focuses on relationships, of professionals, practitioners, young people and their families working together. This is a method of organising services that finds a way for the different knowledges of all involved to have agency and is adaptive and flexible, recognising parents to have changing and differing kinds of needs and to be in a position to negotiate their own preferred identities. Professionals would aim to be 'privilege cognisant' in challenging normative practices. It places the professionals in a range of roles. Instead of understanding what professionals do as enacting a kind of composite expertise around a child, relationships with agencies are seen as supporting the child and their parents in actively becoming the kinds of young people and families they are seeking to be.

Multi-agency working: do we have to use that term?

It is worth unpacking what I mean by 'multi-agency working' and how I propose to talk about it. Disabled children and their families find themselves interacting with a number of different professionals. There may be a need to consult professionals who occupy different roles in health, education, social care and other areas. It is not usually the case that families consult with a single professional – many meet, over time, with a considerable number. Where more than one practitioner or agency is involved there is invariably the question of what kinds of roles are carried out and what kinds of communication is needed in order for them to work effectively with the family; or, to state this another way, that 'multi-agency working' can happen in a range of ways. Furthermore, the manner of such working is experienced by the disabled child and family in a variety of ways, some helpful, some less so. Although I will refer to the term 'multi-agency working' in this chapter, I am not just concerned with the relationships between agencies and how they work together and will therefore aim to challenge certain assumptions. The very term 'multi-agency working' sets up a dynamic of the professionals vis-à-vis children and parents. The focus of this chapter is, therefore, on possibilities for the working relationships between children, young people, parents and professionals. This chapter will not just refer to disabled children, but, in addition, to their parents (subsuming carers) or families, in recognition of the role played by all members of a family in each other's lives and of the particular role that parents of disabled children are often required to play in the life of their child (Mittler and McConachie, 1983; Sandow, 1994a; Gascoigne and Wolfendale, 1995; Wolfendale, 2004). Also, the use of the word 'child' or 'children' will refer to both children and young people.

Multi-agency jigsaw: composite expertise

The call for agencies to work together – and for them to work better together towards a range of goals – is not new. The focus has not, of course, always been solely on the needs of disabled children. For example, the Plowden Report (Department for Education and Science, 1967) saw partnership between professionals as crucial to the solution of the problem of 'social disadvantage'. The same solution was evident in the Court Report (HMSO, 1976) looking at the health needs of all children:

> The real cause of educational failure may lie in the individual's psyche or physical health or in the environment of home, school or society. To disentangle the strands is beyond any single expertise. Medical, social and psychological advice have therefore to be available if the child is to receive the best education that can be offered, and a full team approach with the teacher will sometimes be essential. (HMSO, 1976, section 10.39)

Such thinking goes back even further as demonstrated in an early review, known as the Summerfield Report, of the way educational psychologists operate, encompassing work with disabled children:

> No one discipline can be expert in all aspects of a child's life and the contributions of colleagues trained in the field of psychiatry, psychology, education and the social sciences must all be used effectively, each accepting the competence of his colleagues in their own field. (Department for Education and Science, 1968, section 2.34)

An assumption underlying much past but also present policy and legislation in health, education and social care is that the high level of complexity of problems for some children (not specifically referring to disabled children) has meant that solutions do not lie within any single discipline: that different disciplines make unique contributions.

What we see in these earlier policy developments is the evolution of a model of multi-agency working that has continued to the present. It is a model of differing contributive expertise. This takes a *jigsaw* approach to the individual concerned, seeing the person as separate parts, all with differing needs to be met from the contrasting expertise, skills and knowledges of people from different professional backgrounds. It is the enduring presence of such a rationale that this chapter challenges as having contributed significantly to the failure to make noteworthy headway in improving the ways that agencies work together for and with disabled children and their families.

There is, of course, an obvious face validity to such a 'composite expertise' rationale. It seems clear that there is, in fact, a range of different professional identities, each with arguably dissimilar knowledges and skills, able to help in a number of ways. It follows that working together is about each professional being able to communicate their particular perspectives with respect to the client. Problems in multi-agency working are, therefore, about improving the delivery of services and evolving new systems, and in particular about improving communication. Such conclusions are, indeed, often the outcome of discussions or evaluations in this area (Capper et al, 1993; Kendrick, 1995; Roaf and Lloyd, 1995; Dyson et al, 1998; Easen et al, 2000; Atkinson et al, 2001; Lloyd et al, 2001; Wigfall and Moss, 2001; Roaf, 2002; Stead et al, 2004; Townsley et al, 2004; Brown and White, 2006). However, conceptualising multi-agency working in terms of 'composite expertise' obscures complexities and ambiguities in relationships between agencies and between them and the people with whom they work. Relationships between professionals, and between them and clients, are viewed in logical and linear ways. In particular there is a failure to acknowledge the practices of professionals as having meaning and contributing to the socio-political construction of the identities of children and their families.

If we start to look at multi-professional working through more political lenses, policy developments over the last few decades might yield key understandings. I look at three areas of policy, first, at the genesis of 'special educational needs' through the 1981 Education Act before considering, second, the inclusive education movement. I follow this by looking at the major multi-agency reforms brought about by the Every Child Matters agenda. I then consider the roles in which parents and children have been placed with respect to the professionals, and look at the implications of such relationships, before concluding with some considerations and challenges for more effective relationships. This is a reminder that I am not only looking at 'multi-agency working', as often understood, as what the professionals do and how they communicate and work together, but, moreover, that I am interested in the roles, practices and relationships of professionals, disabled children and their parents, and indeed the wider community.

Warnock: Special educational needs

The 1981 Act, which arose from the Warnock Committee Report (Warnock, 1978), can be seen to have brought multi-agency working to the heart of the statutory assessment of 'special educational needs'. Such involvement of different agencies had not previously been a feature of assessment to the same extent. This Act took away previous labels given to children, which was a clear signal to remove from educational practice the particular kind of deficit thinking associated with these labels. In their place was put the concept of 'need', and in particular 'special educational needs'. Russell (1992) saw the 1981 Education Act as forcing professionals to work together around their differing assessment of need. The increased working together appeared to be a step forward, and, indeed, it did provide improved involvement and accountability in decision-making for a range of professionals. This arguably was progress for disabled children (for those who were given such an assessment), in that the expertise of different professionals was now available in a way that could potentially assist in finding out what was needed within the educational context and making appropriate provision. There was also a possibility that parents might be more involved in assessment, since the Warnock Report was one of the first policy documents to herald parents as partners with professionals (Warnock, 1978).

However, I would not conceptualise the increase in multi-professional involvement as synonymous in any simple way with progress. 'Special educational needs', its concepts, assessment and independent tribunal all assumes an 'individual' and (once again) 'deficit' focus. Attributes understood as internal constructions are assessed and are the basis on which decisions of need and school placement are made. The medical model of disability was invoked, focusing attention away from disability as a construction of society (Barnes, 1981; Oliver, 1996; Shakespeare, 2006). Assessment, intervention and school placement seemed analogous with squeezing differently fashioned pegs into identically shaped holes. There were also 'notions of individualism and progress, combined with a conviction that science was the key to human betterment' (Fisher and Goodley, 2007, p 66). Critique of the educational context, and an investigation of what should change in that context, was avoided. Similarly obscured was debate into the relationship between socio-economic status, poverty and disability, a relationship we know has long existed (Tomlinson, 1982; Sloper, 1999; Blackburn et al, 2010). Significantly, we know that the Warnock Committee was directed away from considering the relationship between poverty and special educational needs (Dyson, 2005).

What was the impact on the role and relationship possibilities for professionals, disabled children and their parents? 'Need', it seemed, provided a way to argue for entitlement. Like motherhood and apple pie, 'need' is not easy to contest. However, need also holds value-laden assumptions and seems to convey notions of empiricism, authority, universality and objectivity. The term appears as something intrinsic to children, rather than '"needs" as extrinsic to children ... "needs" as a cultural construction' (Woodhead, 1991, p 42). Various writers (Edwards, 1978; Fulcher, 1989; Solity, 1991; Wood, 1994; Norwich, 1995) have provided a critique of the currently constructed notion of 'special needs'. As defined in the legislation, special need is a relative concept, defined in relation to educational context and local provision (DfES, 2001). According to the Code of Practice in England (DfES, 2001), a pupil is defined as having special needs if they have a learning difficulty that requires provision to be made, a circular argument. Provision is to be compatible with efficient education for other pupils in the same context. This leads to unresolved ambiguities in the practice of decision-making about individual children. The lack of a clear definition (its circularity, need being what is needed) and the absence of engagement with the politics of need, was a vacuum into which stepped a massive expansion in the number and range of professionals involved (Galloway, 1994), eager to respond to statutory demands to measure and describe the different jigsaw pieces of a child. This refers, of course, to the requirement for psychological, medical and educational advice, required to make decisions about whether to create a statement of special educational needs. Thus the different reports giving alternative perspectives on special needs seemed more an expression of: 'professional ownership, in which medical and educational definitions classify what can be special and who can claim a need' (Corbett, 1993, p 549).

The main role of a multidisciplinary assessment appeared to be to 'provide an arena for these negotiations' (Galloway et al, 1994, p 151). The needs of clients seemed to be 'negotiated between professionals, as well as between professionals and their "clients" in pursuit of a range of professional, political and pragmatic objectives' (Galloway et al, 1994, p 151). It is as if we had created a complex process to describe the emperor's new clothes and then found that the process was problematic, but then continued to spend time making the process work, whilst all the time not realising that, even if it is made less problematic, it may well fail to deliver what is needed.

In conclusion, therefore, 'multi-agency working' created, and became itself, a problem that forever after needed to be addressed. There was (drawing on ideas from activity theory) a runaway quality (Engestrom, 2008); it obscured other solutions and failed to secure effective educational provision for disabled children. I need to make clear at this point that I am not talking here about the intentions of professionals. Working in this arena at the time as an educational psychologist, it was the intention of all those I came across to improve educational experiences for disabled children, as more generally confirmed in the literature (Norwich, 1993; Galloway et al, 1994). What I am referring to here are the ways that practices and structures can work against the intentions of those involved to create unanticipated outcomes. I next discuss whether matters improved as the focus changed towards inclusion.

Inclusive education

The second area considered is that of inclusive education, which has been emerging since the 1980s. Inclusive education is variously defined as to do with the kind of school placement for a child (i.e. mainstream vs special) or more widely and critically:

> as a process of increasing the participation of pupils in, and reducing their exclusion from, the cultures, curricula and communities of their local schools, not forgetting, of course, that education involves many processes that occur outside of schools. (Ainscow, 1999, p 218)

With significant impetus from some parents and professionals, and a strong emerging international lobby (i.e. the Salamanca Statement [UNESCO, 1994]), an inclusion policy imperative started to emerge in the late 1990s with a programme for action and curriculum guidance (Dyson, 2005). In 2001, a Special Educational Needs and Disability Act extended protection on grounds of disability to children in school. At the same time, the Ofsted framework incorporated evaluation of the inclusiveness of schools (Ofsted, 2000). Inclusive education, with its policies and practices, provided a significant change to the aims and focus of much multi-agency work. It changed the kinds of things that professionals expected to achieve in assisting disabled children and their parents with matters to do with schooling and it heralded an increase in multi-agency teams.

Inclusive education has required a departure from the 'known and familiar' and a critique of disabling practices and structures that has not always been easy. However, it has not been fully achieved (Frederickson et al, 2004; Dyson, 2005; Riddell, 2009). It is contentious, resisted by some parents and professionals, under-resourced (though arguably is resource neutral), fails to be achieved for certain groups of young people (Visser and Stokes, 2003), is countered by the standards agenda (the focus on school attainments), and once again is not successful in tackling the more underlying socio-economic problems of the families of disabled children.

On the other hand, the effect of the inclusion movement has been a shift in the context in which needs are assessed. Whilst inclusion *could* take an individual deficit focus and assess what was needed in order to support a child in mainstream education, it opened the way to more debate about the context of education and the extent to which it is disabling. It therefore enabled a more social model of disability to become part of discussions about education and heralded a critique of the school setting in order to bring about a mainstream placement. It was and is still a challenge to the deficit assumptions of the 1981 Act as it focused on looking at how mainstream schools can change to accommodate the needs of the disabled child. One might expect, therefore, less of a focus on deficits. Having been employed as an educational psychologist in a local educational context for parts of the 1980s and 1990s, my impression is that inclusion also brought an increase in the consideration of abilities and personal strengths. This enabled the edging away from the primacy of individual problems and needs. There was, consequently, more attention given to seeking the child's views. Partnership with parents and a consideration of the views of the child were now good practice in assessments (DfES, 2001). The concept of 'special educational needs' did not call for a wider analysis of schools (such as of school improvement or pedagogy, see Dyson, 2005), whereas the concept of inclusion presupposed such an analysis. There was an assumed critique of the professional role that left a space for lobby groups – including the demands of individual parents. With inclusive education, the relationships between disabled children, their parents and professionals seemed tangibly different. However, there remained considerable frustrations for parents in obtaining the services and placements that they were looking for.

Interagency reorganisation: Every Child Matters

More recent policy developments have had further consequences for the shape of the relationships between professionals, disabled children and their families. The Every Child Matters (ECM) (HMSO, 2003) agenda has brought major changes in the way services are structured and organised over the last decade. The overall aim was to improve the social care, education and health of all children, and a structural and financial rearrangement of different agencies, particularly education and social care, was at the heart of these changes. There was a concerted effort for more joined-up thinking and working, reflected in structural changes to services. Professionals were increasingly organised into multi-agency teams. The headline aims for children were those of: being healthy, staying safe, enjoying and achieving, making a positive contribution, and economic well-being. These became guiding principles for health, social and educational services, including schools. Such principles were to be fully compatible with 'inclusive education' in the requirement that 'raising standards in schools and inclusion must go hand in hand' (DfES, 2004, p 36). There was also an obligation to ensure that every child 'has the chance to fulfil their potential by reducing levels of educational failure, ill health, substance abuse and neglect, crime and anti-social behaviour among children and young people' (HMSO, 2003, p 11).

What have been the implications and effects of the ECM agenda on multi-agency working with disabled children? Surely having more integrated multi-agency teams and a focus on improving multi-agency working can only be good? The long-awaited call by parents that the services offered to them should be more 'joined up' seemed, in the ECM agenda, to be within reach. Being joined up meant the achievement of a less stressful negotiation of the involvement of different services, decreasing the time needed to engage a range of practitioners and reducing the need to repeatedly give information (Thomas, 1978; Sandow, 1994b; Roaf and Lloyd, 1995; Dessent, 1996). Key worker roles, as a way to achieve more joined-up services, were central to the changes brought about by the ECM agenda, supported by new developments such as the Common Assessment Framework and the 'team around the child'. However, parents of children have not, it appears, experienced services as more seamless (Abbott et al, 2005b). The key worker role has lacked consistency (Greco and Sloper, 2004) and it does not seem to have been widely available to parents (Townsley et al, 2004; Abbott et al, 2005a; Slade et al, 2009).

There has indeed been an increase in various kinds of provision that has opened up some opportunities for disabled children and their families, such as within Sure Start and Children's Centres and in extended schools and services (Cummings et al, 2005, 2007, 2010; Anning et al, 2006; Stobbs, 2008). A range of interesting and creative projects have been developed. However, the needs of disabled children have to an extent been overlooked. One reason has been the complexity of changes in local authorities that have followed from the ECM agenda (Council for Disabled Children, 2009). The needs of disabled children (and other groups) have been overshadowed, I would claim, by the attention required to improve child safeguarding and protection. This is perhaps not surprising given the origin of the ECM agenda in the tragic death of Victoria Climbié. Furthermore, whilst there is some evidence that professionals themselves have experienced improvements as a result of increased multi-agency working (Abbott et al, 2005a), research suggests that there has not been a commensurate experience of improvement on the part of children and their families. On the contrary, families seem to continue to experience a range of unmet needs (Townsley et al, 2004; Abbott et al, 2005a, 2005b; Goodley, 2007; Slade et al, 2009).

Acknowledgement of the relative failure of the ECM agenda to impact on the lives of disabled children was suggested by the launch of separate initiatives to focus on their needs. For example, *Aiming High for Disabled Children* (AHDC), a joint DfES and HM Treasury report in May 2007 on improving services for disabled children, committed the then government to a 'transformation programme' for the delivery of services for disabled children and their families in England from 2008 to 2011 (HM Treasury, 2007). Other major initiatives have had to make separate calls to make sure that disabled children came within their orbit. For example, the Council for Disabled Children (2009) played a role in trying to ensure that disabled children were catered for within the extended schools and children's centres initiatives, both key to the ECM agenda. Initial indications from pilot projects (i.e. personalisation, individual budgets, person-centred planning) suggested that elements of AHDC had the potential to offer improved multi-agency services for disabled children (Department of Health, 2010). However, they were likely to work well on the assumption that funding would continue beyond the pilot projects.

Another problem was the systemic medical model implicit in the whole edifice of the ECM agenda (Todd, 2007). The key vehicle for achieving the five positive outcomes, with the two overarching tenets of prevention and protection, was the effective offering of services. This could be termed a 'service delivery' emphasis. Effective delivery seemed to be understood in terms of services being offered early enough in places easily accessible to children and families (i.e. in full service extended/integrated schools), delivered by people with the correct skills (workforce reform), and with a graded response so that services were both universal and targeted. There was a well-articulated aim to organise services 'around the child, young person, or family, rather than the existing professional functions' (DfES, 2004). Whilst this seemed all well and good, the focus was again on the individual as in some way needing to be fixed rather than on how problems are produced within a context. It was the professional who does the fixing and it was, once again, most often deficit-focused – the composite expertise model repeatedly in evidence. There were, therefore, contradictory messages for the relationships between children, parents and professionals. On the one hand, improvements were expected given the far-reaching nature of changes that are focused on making multi-agency working work better, but, on the other hand, the systemic medical model that was implicit to the changes strengthened the roles of professionals and arguably made it more difficult for partnership relationships to happen between children, parents and professionals.

Given the advances in multi-agency working expected as a result of the ECM agenda, if improvements were going to happen for disabled children and their families, then it would happen now. However, it seemed that this was not the case.

The story so far

To conclude thus far, the increase in professional involvement in the lives of disabled children post Warnock, the reorganisation of professionals into multi-agency teams as inclusive education came to the fore, and the increasing attention on ways for professionals to work better together in ECM did not seem to have been experienced by children and their parents as making a noticeable and positive impact on their lives. We know that there is long-term evidence of parental dissatisfaction with many educational services and, within this, of the roles of professionals (Thomas, 1978; Piper and Howlin, 1992; Sandow, 1994b; Townsley et al, 2004; Council for Disabled Children, 2009). Such views have not changed greatly throughout the three very different policy developments that have been considered. Indeed, Goodley (2007, p 8) found that 'Parents generally struggle more with coming to terms with fragmented service provision than the "disabilities" of their children'. There have been few attempts to evaluate multi-agency working from the perspective of children. However, we do have some evidence that children have valued some of the contact with professionals for the support provided (Tolley et al, 1998), but have generally not been put in a position where they understood professional roles or how decisions were reached. The main meaning for children of decisions taken about them seemed to be of blame or punishment (Galloway et al, 1994; Armstrong, 1995).

Multi-agency working has consistently been constructed in terms of 'composite expertise'. This appears to have meant that improvements were focused on finding ways to enable the expert to do their work more effectively, or to communicate better with other professionals – or the wholesale and complex reorganisation of local authorities. The solution has been technocratic, managerial and administrative, to find out 'what works' in order to do more of what does, and less of what does not. However, such an analysis militates against alternative, more political and critical, understandings of what happens between parents, children and professionals. It is to these that we turn next.

Constructing identities, positioning roles and knowledge

If the subject matter was uncontested, it is possible that a model of composite expertise might 'work'. However, questions about disability, need, educational provision and health concerns, for example, are rarely in the domain of certainties. They deal with aspects of experience that are socially constructed and contested. Even accepting Shakespeare's (2006) critical realist model of disability (i.e. the understanding that impairments also need to be seen as biological reality rather than solely socio-cultural interaction) the implications for provisions still depend upon the cultural constructions of, for example, education. Roles are unequal in terms of who has permission to speak and to claim knowledge, and when and about what, with the professional usually given the leading role. Our attention is, therefore, drawn to consider different permissions to name and make decisions about what is contested. The dominant individualised, medical model, or deficit focus, of the professional gaze calls for the expert and militates against the involvement of parents and children. This has unintended outcomes. Professional practices together 'form an intricate social process which turns on a series of critical decisions initiating gradual but perceptual changes in a child's social status and leading ultimately to the elaboration of a social role' (Partlett, 1991). McDermott (1996) shows how this can happen in a discussion of the way a child 'is acquired' by a learning difficulty (rather than the other way around). Other authors similarly show practice as social achievement:

... following on from diagnosis, it was left up to the parents to elaborate the idea of subnormality into an organised social role. For these parents, their child bears witness to the social reality of subnormality. From this point onwards, the child's actions and behaviour are assessed as those of someone who is subnormal and thereby work back on themselves to define in turn what subnormality is. (Booth et al, 1991, p 257)

Once this category is attached to a child, those around him or her 'view the child's behaviour as symptoms rather than as expressions of his or her unique personality'. (McLaughlin, 2005, quoting Malloy et al, 2002, p 286)

Objectivist inquiry had produced standardised cultural accounts which tended to subsume the divergent and paradoxical aspects of social living into categories of normalized order. (Danforth, 1995, p 137)

In freezing the image, observational data – already multiply transformed – are set down and become part of the child's history and record. These then become the currency of interchange between professionals' ... little tradition of professionals challenging one another's judgement. (Partlett, 1991, p 229)

It is clear from these quotes that practice is constructive of identities – of children and young people, but also of the parents and even, less obviously, of professionals. The professional role has been one of ownership, placed to define identities of *special need, problem* or *difficulty* and even of *skill* or *resource*. What is implicit is a kind of fixing of the identity claims made by professionals, such that once achieved they are difficult to change.

Whilst the professional role has been one of ownership, active in making identity claims on behalf of children, those same children and their parents have been positioned as passive recipients. This assumed passivity has been the headline story of their role vis-à-vis professionals, alongside other different and contradictory roles and evidence of active engagement in their own lives.

The child has been generally positioned as the 'absent special guest' (Todd, 2007) in all multi-agency decision-making about disabled children. Professional intentions in this area have changed over the last 30 years to bring the child more to the fore. As a result there has been an increase in consultation with children about services, and the involvement of young people in decision-making about their own educational provision (Hobbs et al, 2000). However, much of this activity is tokenistic and naively executed (Arnot and Reay, 2007; Whitty and Wisby, 2008). Professional agendas have continued by and large to drive the questions asked of children in the task of obtaining children's views (Todd, 2007), failing therefore to engage the agency of children. Assumed passivity is challenged by observation of children, showing them to be active in the construction of their own identities (White, 2007). Allen demonstrated the ways that children choose to step both inside and out with respect to their disabled identities as they make sense of the lives they actively engage within:

> One of them got a punishment and Laura didn't, because she's visually impaired. So Laura spoke up and said, "I'd like one too – there's no point in treating me differently because I don't like that". (Allen, 1999, p 63)

Parents occupy simultaneously a number of roles and positions in relation to professionals, alongside an assumed homogeneity. Such positioning is subject to complex trends and discourse, including those from, for example, educational policy, our understandings of disability, childhood, the family and ideas about professional roles. Parents are positioned as passive helpers to the professional, but also as partner, information receiver, consumer and advocate. These exist concurrently and in ways that do not always produce intended and helpful outcomes. 'Passive helper' was dominant in the 1980s (Barton and Moody, 1981; Mittler and McConachie, 1983; Topping, 1986), but seems fully in evidence even in today's integrated services (Townsley et al, 2004; Hodge and Runswick-Cole, 2009), despite the rhetoric (since Warnock) of partnership that has been vocally claimed for the relationship between parents and professionals. Partnership is conditional and not accessible equally to all (Reay, 2004). It is not to be had for those required to supply their child to professionals or those who are 'sent for and told' (Tomlinson, 1981). Even in special schools, parents said their children were not wanted because they did not have 'the right sort of special need' (Duncan, 2003, p 346). Partnership has had unintended outcomes, disempowering by co-opting parents into the professional viewpoint (Galloway et al, 1994; Armstrong, 1995).

The growing neo-liberalism of the 1980s has had clients and patients now renamed consumers. Societal strikes on the professional role (i.e.

increasing accountability) has brought about the advocate model, with expectations that parents will be asked their views and make demands about service quality (Bastiani, 1987; Sandow et al, 1987; McCarthy, 1991; Armstrong, 1995). In such a context, the existence of powerful pressure groups behind certain types of special educational need has led to advantages for some parents (but not all) in terms of securing scarce educational resources (Riddell et al, 1994, p 342).

The notion of parents as passive recipients of services has been challenged by evidence that they are active in response to disability, 'actively involved in conceptualizing and enacting care with their (disabled) babies' (Goodley and Tregaskis, 2006, p 643). As with children, there is evidence that parents seek both to step into a narrative of disability for their child, and also at other times to step outside this narrative:

> Every second of his day, I was trying to teach him something. Everything had got a target about it ... but, recently I've thought 'just love him'. I can't keep chasing that normal, normal. I feel I've done so much to try and make him normal. I just can't keep that up. I need to accept him as he is and enjoy him as he is. (Fisher and Goodley, 2007, p 76)

> They seek to ensure that their child does not become contained, categorized, subjectified within a diagnosis; a false home disallowing other possibilities for the child's progress. (McLaughlin and Goodley, 2008, p 327)

The complex politics by which children and parents are often silenced is also reductionist about the professional role. For example, educational psychologists variously see themselves as partners, advocates, informed facilitators, researchers, theorists, problem solvers and listeners, to name a few (Sykes et al, 2008). In a critical analysis of partnership the educational psychologist saw her role as 'bleaching the arena of blame' (Todd, 2000). I do not have space to discuss the role complexities of other professionals likely to be working with disabled children. However, such professional identities are a long way from taking the lead in constructing identities or from standing in the way of partnership. Once again, to unravel such politics is not simply about improving structures or communication between different professional groups. These roles are obscured by the normative social practices and identity achievements of, for example, assessment and intervention.

Conclusion: 'privilege cognisant' professional to facilitate active becoming

To avoid another 30 years in which well-meaning and hard-working professionals struggle to work effectively and to remove the need for the great effort of parents to secure services and provision, a change of direction is needed. Professionals need to start to engage with practice as politics and as a social and identity-forming achievement. There should also be a focus on the relationships between professionals, parents and children. For the Conservative–Liberal Democrat Coalition government there is a challenge as to how to maintain this focus in the context of their expected emphasis on attainment and on special provision. The option, contained in the Green Paper on education for disabled children and children with special educational needs (Department for Education, 2011), for personal budgets for families may help to place parents more in a position of agency in relationships with professionals.

As to the exact form that such a relational focus should take, the problem for commissioners of services is that a political analysis does not seem to lead to clear definitions of 'what works' and 'best practice'. My analysis, however, suggests certain aspects that might need to be present. An exploration with children and families together to evolve local services would be a good place to start, bearing in mind what we know about the political pitfalls of partnership and consultation, as discussed earlier in this chapter. My 'people, practice, context' (PPC) model of partnership (Todd, 2007) suggests the need for a critique of practice, and an evolution in the role of the professional. Professionals should aim to be 'privilege cognisant' (Bailey, 2008) to challenge and uncover normative practices. They need to be able to step into the expert role when required, but to abandon it at other times in favour of what Fisher and Goodley (2007, p 68) refer to as 'the philosophy of the present and becoming'. Similarly:

> The parent–professional relationship needs to be fluid, able to respond to changing perspectives and shifting perspectives as parents and professionals engage with new experiences and influences. Those professionals who engage with parents as guides, experts on their children who can identify the skills as well as the deficits, are trusted and well received. It is the professionals who are willing to learn about the child, rather than those who want only to know about the

'disability', who are able to work effectively as partners. (Hodge and Runswick-Cole, 2009, p 654)

Finally, I claim that it is the professional's responsibility to make the first move to create a space where all knowledges, those of children, parents and professionals, are not just stated, but have agency.

References
Abbott, D., Townsley, R. and Watson, D. (2005a) 'Multi-Agency Working in Services for Disabled Children: What Impact Does It Have on Professionals?', *Health and Social Care in the Community*, vol 13, pp 155–63.

Abbott, D., Watson, D. and Townsley, R. (2005b) 'The Proof of the Pudding: What Difference Does Multi-Agency Working Make to Families with Disabled Children with Complex Health Care Needs?', *Child and Family Social Work*, vol 10, pp 229–38.

Ainscow, M. (1999) *Understanding the Development of Inclusive Schools*, London: Falmer.

Allen, J. (1999) *Actively Seeking Inclusion: Pupils with Special Needs in Mainstream Schools*, London: Falmer Press.

Anning, A., Cottrell, D. M., Frost, N., Green, J. and Robinson, M. (2006) *Developing Multiprofessional Teamwork for Integrated Children's Services*, Buckingham: Open University Press.

Armstrong, D. (1995) *Power and Partnership in Education*, London: Routledge.

Arnot, M. and Reay, D. (2007) 'A Sociology of Pedagogic Voice: Power, Inequality and Pupil Consultation', *Discourse: Studies in the Cultural Politics of Education*, vol 28, pp 311–25.

Atkinson, M., Wilkin, A., Stott, A. and Kinder, K. (2001) *Multi-Agency Working: An Audit of Activity. LGA Research Report 17*, Slough: NFER.

Bailey, A. (2008) 'Locating Traitorous Identities: Towards a Privilege Cognizant White Character', in A. Bailey and C. Cuomo (eds) *The Feminist Philosophy Reader*, New York: McGraw-Hill.

Barnes, C. (1981) *Disabled People in Britain and Discrimination: A Case for Anti-Discrimination Legislation*, London: Hurst.

Barton, L. and Moody, S. (1981) 'The Value of Parents to the ESN(S) School: An Examination', in L. Barton and S. Tomlinson (eds) *Special Education: Policy, Practices and Social Issues*, London: Harper and Row.

Bastiani, J. (ed) (1987) *Parents and Teachers 1: Perspectives on Home–School Relations*, Windsor: NFER-Nelson.

Blackburn, C. M., Spencer, N. J. and Read, J. M. (2010) 'Prevalence of Childhood Disability and the Characteristics and Circumstances of Disabled Children in the UK: Secondary Analysis of the Family Resources Survey', *BioMedCentral Pediatrics*, vol 10, pp 1–12.

Booth, T., Masterson, M., Potts, P. and Swann, W. (eds) (1991) *Policies for Diversity in Education*, London: Routledge.

Brown, K. and White, K. (2006) *Exploring the Evidence Base for Integrated Children's Services*, Edinburgh: Scottish Executive Education Department.

Capper, C., Hanson, S. and Huilman, R. R. (1993) 'Community-Based Interagency Collaboration: A Poststructural Interpretation of Critical Practices', *Journal of Educational Policy*, vol 9, pp 335–51.

Corbett, J. (1993) 'Postmodernism and the "Special Needs" Metaphors', *Oxford Review of Education*, vol 19, pp 547–54.

Council for Disabled Children (2009) *Every Disabled Child Matters. Disabled Children and Health*, Campaign briefing, June 2009, London: National Children's Bureau.

Cummings, C., Dyson, A., Jones, L., Laing, K. and Todd, L. (2010) *Extended Services Evaluation. Reaching Disadvantaged Groups and Individuals. Thematic Review*, London: Department for Children, Schools and Families.

Cummings, C., Dyson, A., Papps, I., Pearson, D., Raffo, C. and Todd, L. (2005) *Evaluation of the Full Service Extended Schools Project: End of First Year Report*, London: DfES.

Cummings, C., Dyson, A., Muijs, D., Papps, I., Pearson, P., Raffo, C., Tiplady, L. and Todd, L. (2007) *Evaluation of the Full Service Extended Schools Initiative: Final Report*, Research Report 852, London: DfES.

Danforth, S. (1995) 'Towards a Critical Theory Approach to Lives Considered Emotionally Disturbed', *Behavioural Disorders*, vol 20, pp 136–43.

Department for Education (2011) *Support and Aspiration: A New Approach to Special Educational Needs and Disability: A Consultation*, Norwich: TSO.

Department for Education and Science (1967) *Children and their Primary Schools: A Report of the Central Advisory Council for Education (England) Volume 1: The Report*, London: HMSO.

Department for Education and Science (1968) *Psychologists in Education Services. Report of a Working Party Appointed by the Secretary of State for Education and Science: The Summerfield Report*, London: HMSO.

Department of Health (2010) *Person Centred Planning, March 2010*, London: Department of Health.

Dessent, T. (1996) 'Meeting Special Educational Needs – Options for Partnership between Health, Social and Education Services', in S.P.O.S. Group (ed) *Options for Partnership between Health, Education and Social Services*, Tamworth: NASEN.

DfES (Department for Education and Skills) (2001) *Special Educational Needs Code of Practice*, London: DFES.

DfES (2004) *Every Child Matters: Next Steps*, London: DfES.

Duncan, N. (2003) 'Awkward Customers? Parents and Provision for Special Educational Needs', *Disability and Society*, vol 18, pp 341–56.

Dyson, A. (2005) 'Philosophy, Politics and Economics? The Story of Inclusive Education in England', in D. Mitchell (ed) *Contextualising Inclusive Education: Evaluating Old and New International Perspectives*, London: Routledge.

Dyson, A., Lin, M. and Millward, A. (1998) *Effective Communication between Schools, LEAs and Health and Social Services in the Field of Special Educational Needs*, London: DfEE.

Easen, P., Atkins, M. and Dyson, A. (2000) 'Inter-professional Collaboration and Conceptualisations of Practice', *Children and Society*, vol 14, pp 355–67.

Edwards, J. (1978) 'Comment on Warnock. 1. Is the concept of "need" justified?', *Association of Educational Psychologists Journal*, vol 4, pp 44–5.

Engestrom, Y. (2008) 'The Future of Activity Theory: A Rough Draft', paper presented at 'ISCAR 2008 – Ecologies of Diversities: The Developmental and Historical Interarticulation of Human Mediational Forms', San Diego, California, US.

Fisher, P. and Goodley, D. (2007) 'The Linear Medical Model of Disability: Mothers of Disabled Babies Resist with Counter-Narratives', *Sociology of Health and Illness*, vol 29, pp 66–81.

Frederickson, N., Dunsmuir, S., Lang, J. and Monsen, J. (2004) 'Mainstream–Special School Inclusion Partnerships: Pupil, Parent and Teacher Perspectives', *International Journal of Inclusive Education*, vol 8, pp 37–57.

Fulcher, G. (1989) *Disabling Policies? A Comparative Approach to Educational Policy and Disability*, London and New York: Falmer Press.

Galloway, D. (1994) 'The Role of Consultants in Reviewing Provision for Special Educational Needs: Cautionary Tales', *Evaluation and Research in Education*, vol 8, pp 97–107.

Galloway, D., Armstrong, D. and Tomlinson, S. (1994) *The Assessment of Special Educational Needs: Whose Problem?* Harlow: Longman.

Gascoigne, E. and Wolfendale, S. (1995) *Working with Parents as Partners in SEN*, London: David Fulton.

Goodley, D. (2007) *Parents, Professionals and Disabled Babies: Identifying Enabling Care: Non-Technical Summary (Research Summary)*. ESRC End of Award Report, RES-000-23-0129, Swindon: ESRC.

Goodley, D. and Tregaskis, C. (2006) 'Storying Disability and Impairment: Retrospective Accounts of Disabled Family Life', *Qualitative Health Research*, vol 16, pp 630–46.

Greco, V. and Sloper, P. (2004) 'Care Co-Ordination and Key Worker Schemes for Disabled Children: Results of a UK-Wide Survey', *Child: Care, Health and Development*, vol 30, pp 13–20.

HMSO (1976) *Fit for the Future. Report of the Committee on Child Health Services*, London: HMSO.

HMSO (2003) *Every Child Matters*, London: HMSO.

HM Treasury (2007) *Aiming High for Disabled Children: Better Support for Families*, London: HM Treasury and DfES.

Hobbs, C., Taylor, J. and Todd, L. (2000) 'Consulting with Children and Young People. Enabling Educational Psychologists to Work Collaboratively with Children and Young People', *Educational and Child Psychology*, vol 17, pp 107–15.

Hodge, N. and Runswick-Cole, K. (2009) 'Problematising Parent–Professional Partnerships in Education', *Disability and Society*, vol 23, pp 637–47.

Kendrick, A. (1995) 'Supporting Families through Inter-Agency Work: Youth Strategies in Scotland', in M. Mill, R. K. Hawthorne and D. Part (eds) *Supporting Families*, Edinburgh: HMSO.

Lloyd, G., Stead, J. and Kendrick, A. (2001) *Hanging on in There. a Study of Inter-Agency Work to Prevent School Exclusion in Three Local Authorities*, London: National Children's Bureau.

McCarthy, T. (1991) 'Children with Special Educational Needs: Parents' Knowledge of Procedures and Provisions', *British Journal of Special Education*, vol 18, pp 17–19.

McDermott, R.P. (1996) 'The Acquisition of a Child by a Learning Disability', in S. Chaiklin and J. Lave (eds) *Understanding Practice. Perspectives on Activity and Context*, Cambridge: Cambridge University Press.

McLaughlin, J. (2005) 'Exploring Diagnostic Processes: Social Science Perspectives', *Archives of Disease in Childhood*, vol 90, pp 284–7.

McLaughlin, J. and Goodley, D. (2008) 'Seeking and Rejecting Certainty: Exposing the Sophisticated Lifeworlds of Parents of Disabled Babies', *Sociology*, vol 42, pp 317–35.

Mittler, P. and McConachie, H. (1983) *Parents, Professionals and Mentally Handicapped People: Approaches to Partnership*, London: Croom Helm.

Norwich, B. (1993) 'Ideological Dilemmas in Special Needs Education: Practitioners' Views', *Oxford Review of Education*, vol 19, pp 527–46.

Norwich, B. (1995) 'Statutory Assessment and Statementing: Some Challenges and Implications for Educational Psychologists', *Educational Psychology in Practice*, vol 11, pp 29–35.

Ofsted (2000) *Evaluating Educational Inclusion: Guidance for Inspectors and Schools HMI 235*, London: Ofsted.

Oliver, M. (1996) *Understanding Disability: From Theory to Practice*, Basingstoke: Macmillan.

Partlett, M. (1991) 'The Assessment of Hearing-Impaired Children', in D. Schon (ed) *The Reflective Turn: Case Studies in and on Educational Practice*, New York: Teachers College Press.

Piper, E. and Howlin, P. (1992) 'Assessing and Diagnosing Developmental Disorders That are not Evident at Birth: Parental Evaluations of Intake Procedures', *Child: Care, Health and Development*, vol 18, pp 35–55.

Reay, D. (2004) 'Educational and Cultural Capital: The Implications of Changing Trends in Education Policies', *Cultural Trends*, vol 13, pp 73–86.

Riddell, S. (2009) 'Social Justice, Equality and Inclusion in Scottish Education', *Discourse: Studies in the Cultural Politics of Education*, vol 30, pp 283–96.

Riddell, S., Brown, S. and Duffield, J. (1994) 'Parental Power and Special Educational Needs: The Case of Specific Learning Difficulties', *British Educational Research Journal*, vol 20, pp 327–44.

Roaf, C. (2002) *Co-ordinating Services for Included Children: Joined Up Action*, Buckingham: Open University Press.

Roaf, C. and Lloyd, C. (1995) *Multi-Agency Work with Young People in Difficulty*, York: Joseph Rowntree Foundation.

Russell, P. (1992) 'Boundary Issues: Multidisciplinary Working in New Contexts – Implications for Educational Psychology Practice', in S. Wolfendale (ed) *The Profession and Practice of Educational Psychology*, London: Cassell.

Sandow, S. (1994a) 'They Told me he would be a Vegetable: Parent's Views', in S. Sandow (ed) *Whose Special Need? Some Perceptions of Special Educational Needs*, London: Paul Chapman.

Sandow, S. (ed) (1994b) *Whose Special Need? Some Perceptions of Special Educational Needs*, London: Paul Chapman.

Sandow, S., Stafford, D. and Stafford, P. (1987) *An Agreed Understanding? Parent–Professional Communication and the 1981 Education Act*, Windsor: NFER-Nelson.

Shakespeare, T. (2006) *Disability Rights and Wrongs*, London: Routledge.

Slade, Z., Coulter, A. and Joyce, L. (2009) *Parental Experience of Services for Disabled Children*, Research Report DCSF-RR147, August 2009, London: BMRB Qualitative.

Sloper, P. (1999) 'Models of Service Support for Parents of Disabled Children. What Do We Know? What Do We Need to Know?', *Child: Care, Health and Development*, vol 25, pp 85–99.

Solity, J. E. (1991) 'Special Needs: A Discriminatory Concept?', *Educational Psychology in Practice*, vol 7, pp 12–19.

Stead, J., Lloyd, G. and Kendrick, A. (2004) 'Participation or Practice Innovation: Tensions in Inter-Agency Working to Address Disciplinary Exclusion from School', *Children and Society*, vol 18, pp 42–52.

Stobbs, P. (2008) *Extending Inclusion. Access for Disabled Children and Young People to Extended Schools and Children's Centres: A Development Manual*, Nottingham: Council for Disabled Children.

Sykes, G., Todd, L., Carson, S., Dhir, G. and Gilbert, S. (2008) *Clarifying and Developing the Role of the EP in Relation to All Aspects of Parent and Carer Partnership, Advocacy and Training. Executive Summary, DECP Parent Partnership Working Party Report*, Leicester: British Psychological Society.

Thomas, D. (1978) *The Social Psychology of Childhood Disability*, London: Methuen.

Todd, E. S. (2000) 'The Problematic of Partnership in the Assessment of Special Educational Needs', PhD Thesis, Newcastle University.

Todd, L. (2007) *Partnerships for Inclusive Education: A Critical Approach to Collaborative Working*, London: Routledge.

Tolley, E., Girma, M., Stanton-Wharmby, A., Spate, A. and Milburn, J. (1998) *Young Opinions, Great Ideas*, London: National Children's Bureau.

Tomlinson, S. (1981) *Educational Subnormality: A Study in Decision Making*, London: Routledge and Kegan Paul.

Tomlinson, S. (1982) *A Sociology of Special Education*, London: Routledge and Kegan Paul.

Topping, K. (1986) *Parents as Educators: Training Parents to Teach Their Children*, London: Croom Helm.

Townsley, R., Abbott, D. and Watson, D. (2004) *Making a Difference? Exploring the Impact of Multi-agency Working on Disabled Children with Complex Health Care Needs, Their Familiies and the Professionals Who Support Them*, Bristol: The Policy Press.

UNESCO (1994) *The Salamanca Statement and Framework for Action on Special Needs Education*, Paris: UNESCO.

Visser, J. and Stokes, S. (2003) 'Is Education Ready for the Inclusion of Pupils with Emotional and Behavioural Difficulties: A Rights Perspective?', *Educational Review*, vol 55, pp 65–75.

Warnock, M. (1978) *Report of the Committee of Enquiry into the Education of Handicapped Children and Young People*, London: HMSO.

White, M. (2007) *Maps of Narrative Practice*, London: Norton.

Whitty, G. and Wisby, E. (2008) 'Whose Voice? An Exploration of the Current Policy Interest in Pupil Involvement in School Decision-Making', *International Studies in Sociology of Education*, vol 17, pp 303–19.

Wigfall, V. and Moss, P. (2001) *More Than the Sum of Its Parts? A Study of a Multi-Agency Child Care Network?* London: National Children's Bureau.

Wolfendale, S. (2004) 'Getting the Balance Right: Towards Partnership in Assessing Children's Development and Educational Achievement', Discussion paper commissioned by DfES, London: DfES. Available at: www.teachernet.gov.uk/workingwithparents

Wood, K. (1994) 'Towards National Criteria for Special Educational Needs: Some Conceptual and Practical Considerations for Educational Psychologists', *Educational Psychology in Practice*, vol 10, pp 85–92.

Woodhead, M. (1991) 'Psychology and the Cultural Construction of "Children's Needs"', in M. Woodhead, P. Light and R. Carr (eds) *Growing Up in a Changing Society*, London: Routledge, Open University.

FIVE

Disabled children's 'voice' and experiences

Ann Lewis

'Voice' matters, not primarily for legal, rights or procedural reasons, but because it connects with a fundamental human urge to communicate the narratives of our lives and in so doing foster understanding and compassion. This chapter is written from the underlying perspective that all children,[1] with or without disabilities or special needs,[2] have a right to have their views (narratives) heard and to be asked about matters concerning them. Progress in consulting with disabled children has lagged behind that of formally seeking children's views more generally. This was recognised by Morris (2003) and Gray (2002), who noted the paucity of information obtained directly from disabled children and young people.

However, the first decade of the 21st century saw a widening body of work that involves hearing the views of children, including disabled children, and when consultation has taken place in authentic ways we can see genuine improvements in provision. For example, the development of inclusive libraries (e.g. the explicit inclusion of materials accessible to people with severe learning difficulties) has been triggered as a response to the demands from disabled people (Lacey, forthcoming). This positive outcome would not have been realised without the seeking of views being considered as a possibility, appropriate opportunities provided to communicate views and, in turn, these views being understood and acted upon.

In this chapter, I examine the fine grain of facilitating the voice of disabled children, particularly in the research context (with implications for other contexts). First, I review some ethical ground rules for consulting with disabled children. Second, I discuss various methods, developed across a range of research and evaluation projects, for facilitating such consultation. Third, I summarise some key messages about what it is that disabled children are telling us, through such processes, about their lives and experiences. Running through this material is the overriding importance of a listening culture. This listening culture encompasses, in the research context, emancipatory as well as participatory approaches in which the children involved are co-researchers researched with, rather than 'researched on' (Grover, 2004; Walmsley, 2005).

Background and cautions

Consulting with children, including disabled children, was encapsulated in Article 12 of the United Nations Convention on the Rights of the Child (UNCRC), ratified by the UK in 1991. However, the UNCRC has not been incorporated into English law. Thus, individual children cannot invoke Article 12 and so secure their autonomy rights through the courts (Potter, 2008). Interestingly, the Lamb Inquiry (DCSF, 2009a) recommended that, drawing on disability legislation, children themselves (not just their parents) should have the right to appeal to the SEN Tribunal. Aside from these legal points, the importance of exploring children's own views, including those of disabled children, has been recognised across the policy, research and practice of children's services' (Save the Children, 2001; DCSF, 2009a).

This progress masks a hazy diversity of practice (and rationale) across a spectrum ranging from 'listening', 'involvement' and 'participation', through 'consultation', to 'co-collaboration'. The various terms echo Hart's (1992) much-quoted (and simplified) eight-step ladder of participation (from manipulation, through decoration and tokenism, to, eventually, child-initiated participation with decisions shared with adults). The last is a very radical position, as indicated by the following speaker: "Adults have to accept the fact that they are losing power; but they need reassurance and reinforcement that we can use power constructively if we share it".[3] In contrast, Marcel Berlins (2008), a lawyer, commented: "Children do not always or, indeed, usually, know what's good for them, or for other children. That's why we have adults." So, despite a growing pro-voice movement, strong differences of opinion remain about the desirability, feasibility and limits in implementing the principle of child voice.

Scrutiny of how the principle of disabled children's voice has been translated into practice suggests that while considerable progress has been made in rights-based arguments and in developing approaches, there has been a blurring of purpose, insufficient regard to ethical issues and an overemphasis on procedures. Reflecting these points, a series of commentators have taken a more critical look at child 'voice' as well as consultation with children in general (Fielding, 2004; Komulainen, 2007; Lewis 2010).

Slippage between principle and practice is evident. The purposes behind promoting consultation with children are highly varied, and some are at variance with one another. For example, within schools, the promotion of voice may be used as a vehicle through which to promote 'active citizenship', for example, involving pupils in school councils (School Councils UK, 2005). Seen positively, this may well lead to improved provision. For example, in one case study of a School Council in a special school for pupils with severe or profound learning/communication difficulties, severely disabled children used augmentative communication aids via classmates to share their views (including concerning access issues in the city centre). In another special school, the School Council was instrumental in changing practice at lunchtimes, leading to wider meal choices and more flexible organisation of seating (Lewis et al, 2007). These examples show pupils contributing genuinely to direction within, and beyond, the school although stopping short of radical change. However, they also convey how constrained child 'voice' is likely to be when operating within conventional and essentially conservative structures.

Another aspect of the possible usurping of child voice is linked to the monitoring and inspection of professionals and services. This is illustrated well in the national Ofsted Tellus survey (annually from 2007), which asks children about their local area 'in order to ensure that the first-hand views of children and young people are taken into account as part of each local authority's inspection process, and to provide data to compare at a national level'.[4] Concerns about this use of child 'voice' are reinforced by the DCSF wording of the associated research contract (December 2009). This contract notes the importance of the survey providing 'robust time series data that can be used to measure performance against specified DCSF owned, national and PSA indicators'.[5] These purposes conspicuously lack reference to the intrinsic value and listening culture behind the rationale of 'voice'.

Some ethical issues in hearing the views of disabled children

Vulnerable interviewees, including some disabled children, are likely to invest a great deal in the encounter through which their views are sought when this is approached authentically. This may also be true of the professionals or researchers involved, particularly where the seeking of views is sustained over time (Booth, 1998; Crozier and 'Tracey', 2000). Similarly, involvement in steering, reference or advisory groups, while highly productive in many ways, may be difficult for participants in terms of sustaining relationships and expectations. One solution is to maintain a research reference group of disabled children and young people (e.g. at university or organisational level) whose involvement is regularly sought and costed into proposals (Porter et al, 2005; Lewis et al, 2008).

A specific focus on disability (e.g. what do *disabled* children feel about their out-of-school activities? How do the views of *disabled* children and the views of their parents compare?) may give overriding importance to one aspect – the child's disability. This may provide an unwelcome overemphasis of this aspect of the child at the expense of more important (to the child) personal characteristics such as age, gender, position in the family, personality or interests. It is striking that research into the views of disabled children (see the 'Findings' section later) points overwhelmingly to the insignificance of their disability, in itself, compared with the emphasis on commonalities with other children (e.g. desire for independence, friendships and the fostering of shared interests, such as sports or music).

Gatekeepers

At a local level and in the research context, one set of gatekeepers when hoping to consult with disabled children are research ethics committees. Partly with these in mind, professional bodies (e.g. BERA, BPS, BSA) have developed ethical guidelines in relation to research and practice with potentially vulnerable people. Such guidelines make reference to various matters concerning gatekeepers as well as consent, confidentiality and ownership. The guidelines reflect a broad consensus among a particular group at a given time and need to be interpreted flexibly, referenced to the underlying ethos rather than adherence to technicalities (Morrow, 2008).

The limited systematic evidence concerning the operation and impact of ethical protocols with children suggests that their effectiveness and value is questionable in some respects. For example, reassuring children about confidentiality, or the nuances of fully informed consent, is futile if children do not understand and/or believe these protocols (Hurley and Underwood, 2002).

Several reports have highlighted the ways in which NHS ethics procedures may hold up research inappropriately and ultimately be counterproductive (Stalker et al, 2004; Scott et al, 2006). It is ironic that such procedures or committees may, by being too inflexible, silence the very people whom they were intended to 'protect' and give a voice. For example, at the time of writing, clarification is being sought concerning the 2005 Mental Capacity Act (MCA). The Act applies to individuals of 16 years of age or over who lack the capacity to consent. Only the lengthy NHS ethics committees have the authorisation to sanction research under the remit of the MCA (whether inside or outside the NHS) (see www.legislation.gov.uk/ukpga/2005/9/contents). This would seem likely to stop or curb modest and smaller projects (such as those conducted by professionals in training) that involve hearing the views of some disabled children (e.g. those on the autistic spectrum or with learning disabilities).

Whether parental consent must be obtained when seeking children's views has been the subject of debate (Masson, 2000). Connolly (2008) working with socially excluded young people with challenging behaviour encountered a variety of practices with some head teachers requiring her to contact parents and others not doing so. This variability may be judged as helpful and individualised, but it may put in jeopardy such young people's intrinsic right to have their views heard. In some contexts, adult gatekeepers (such as head teachers) will provide an 'all in' access; for example, when a head teacher agrees to all children being interviewed and this is construed as part of the usual school curriculum.

In contrast, adult gatekeepers may operate an 'opt in' policy. Alderson and Morrow (2004) argue that this is exclusionary because opting in requires certain skills (e.g. communication) and attitudes (e.g. confidence). Similarly, some parents of children with severe learning difficulties argue that their children lack the communication skills to make their views known, and so their children are seriously disadvantaged in any system that prioritises child voice (DCSF, 2009a). This position (although understandable) gives prominence to a parental gatekeeping role rather than addressing authentic ways in which the children's views may be ascertained.

Confidentiality and the ethics of openness

Some workers involved in consulting with children argue that it is not advisable or useful to make guarantees of confidentiality as there is always the possibility that information (e.g. suspected abuse), which the interviewer has a moral duty to forward, may be revealed. This is highly relevant given the co-occurrence of disability and disadvantage. Disabled children are over-represented among children who:

- experience physical or sexual abuse (Westcott and Jones, 1999);
- are bullied – particularly so for children with learning difficulties (DCSF, 2009a);

- take illicit drugs or alcohol – particularly so for children with learning difficulties (DCSF, 2009b);
- are temporarily excluded from school – particularly so for children with emotional or behavioural difficulties (DCSF, 2009b);
- are recurrently absent from school – particularly so for boys (DCSF, 2009b);
- live in poverty (Emerson and Hatton, 2007);
- are being 'looked after' – that is, in care (Potter, 2008); and
- are in homes characterised by family break-up (Potter, 2008).

Conversely, some disabled children explicitly want their views known more widely. In that case, guarantees about confidentiality may be counterproductive. This clarification about the nature and purpose of the consultation is critical and links with research ownership and epistemology. These have implications for children's potential involvement in dissemination events, which give them a chance to publicly own the data and findings. In one project, researchers returned documents (posters and diary records) to participants (with learning difficulties) to underline children's ownership of these, but this action was interpreted by the children as rejection of those materials as being too poor for adults' retention or public display. These points highlight again the importance of a listening culture and the need to be aware that the child's perspective may be radically different from that of the adult. As a result of the increasing recognition of these subtleties, there is a growing tendency to offer anonymity (i.e. the child will not be identifiable by name), but neither offer nor guarantee confidentiality.

Through assent to fully informed consent

The continuum from fully informed consent, through assent, to failure to object highlights the distinction between consent and assent. Alderson and Morrow (2004) argue that fully informed consent is the ideal. In order to give fully informed consent the child providing this has to have: information about the chance to participate, knowledge about a right to withdraw from the activity and the nature of the participant's role, plus understanding about intended outcomes. To be able to respond to all these aspects of fully informed consent, the child (or someone on their behalf) has to receive the information, understand it and respond to it. Elaborated in this way it can be seen that obtaining fully informed consent may be a considerable and possibly daunting undertaking. We should be frank about how difficult it may be to obtain fully informed consent (Clegg, 2004) within even emancipatory and participatory approaches.

Less robustly, consent may be given by the child or by another on the child's behalf for (a) the child to be consulted or (b) the adult to invite the child to share their views. *Assent* refers to the child's agreement to participation in the process when another has given consent. In the more conventional context of consulting with adults these two aspects are conflated, that is, the adult being consulted both consents and assents to the interview. The two types of agreement may be conflated, but disentangling them highlights the way in which a succession of consents on behalf of children, particularly those with learning difficulties, may profoundly influence sampling and hence findings. If the consent/assent processes are distinct, then after consent by others has been given, the child needs to give assent to participation. Further along the continuum of consent, Alderson and Morrow (2004) note the importance of allowing informed *dissent* by the child.

It is unusual to read of the detailed outcomes of consent processes. Exceptions include work with disabled children by Cameron and Murphy (2007), Beresford et al (2004), Connolly (2008) and Snelgrove (2005), all involving people with learning difficulties. Snelgrove provides a careful discussion of consent and coercion in research involving children with moderate or severe learning difficulties. This includes an account of procedures concerning withdrawal from the research (and the possibility of an independent witness to this) as well as checks that the children knew how to decline involvement. 'In a field where research participants are recognised as a vulnerable group, documenting non-participation rates is vital' (Cameron and Murphy, 2007, p 116). The various strategies through which children may withdraw fully or partially from consultation deserve much wider discussion and scrutiny.

Allowing/encouraging silence

Matters of consent raise questions about silence. An opting in to consultation is simultaneously an opting out of silence. Some practices may inadvertently put undue pressure on children to continue participation (e.g. the use of various incentives/rewards for participation; the location of interviews; introduction to the consultation in ways that reinforce adult–child power relationships). Accounts of the consultation processes need to problematise such incentives, especially as participation may not be in the children's best interests (Roberts, 2000). The special educational needs/disability field is conspicuous in beginning to test and demonstrate claims about the use of ethical protocols. This reflects the testing of methodological boundaries because assumptions concerning capabilities, applied to other children, cannot be made so readily (Lewis and Porter, 2004, 2007).

A preference by children for silence, despite elaborate ethical protocols and careful procedures to facilitate their voicing of views, warrants more notice. At one level it is merely a more clear statement of reality: the best ethical protocols and sensitive methods will still only generate a partial picture of children's worlds. Whatever data are collected, and whatever conclusions are drawn, much remains undisclosed. It would make the work more transparent if all activities involving 'child voice' included an explicit account of whether, why and how children's silences were recognised, noted, responded to and interpreted (Lewis, 2010).

Sharing views – methods

There is a very close and two-way relationship between how disabled children's views are obtained (methods) and whose views are sought (sampling). Individual methods facilitate particular types of responses and hence include or exclude certain children. Conversely, the wish to include specific children (or groups) will prompt particular choices about methods, possibly including the tailored development of preferred approaches. Thus, the chosen way of communicating (ideally the result of a researcher–researched conversation) shapes who 'hears' whom (both ways: researcher–researched; see earlier concerning participatory approaches).

A vast array of methods-related materials are available in relation to disabled children and voice. These encompass:

- materials relevant to all children (e.g. Kirby et al, 2003);
- resources from campaigning groups for children (e.g. A National Voice, Article 12, Young Voice, CRIN, Childline, Council for Disabled Children, Save the Children);
- empirical projects involving exploration of disabled children's voice (e.g. Davis et al, 2000; Connors and Stalker, 2003; Lewis et al, 2007; Sloper et al, 2009);
- approaches concerning voice, developed specifically through research with disabled children (e.g. Beresford et al, 2004, 2007);
- development work involving voice and disabled children (e.g. Marchant and Jones, 2003; Aitken and Millar, 2004; Watson et al, 2007; Byers et al, 2008); and

- critiques concerning disability and child voice (e.g. Stone, 2001; Cocks, 2008; Franklin and Sloper, 2009; Nind, 2009).

The overall conclusions concerning effective methods when consulting with disabled children are that: the encounter needs to be genuine; 'one size will not fit all', methods have to be adjusted to the individual child's needs and preferences; and a portfolio of methods through which various approaches are developed with each child is likely to be more useful than researcher- (or sponsor-)determined 'one-shot' approaches. These may be regarded as applicable to all children, but are particularly significant for disabled children.

Do disabled children require different methods when sharing 'voice' from those used with other children? Disabled children are heterogeneous, but aside from the inevitable human variability, there are some generalisable disability-related pointers. If an ethos of a listening culture pervades the exploration of voice, then disabled children will be able to guide the researchers about useful modifications, whether these are related to disability or other features of the context. Disability-oriented guidance, in particular, needs to be interpreted reflectively, as otherwise it may constrain thinking about methods.

Given those cautions, some children, notably those with autism spectrum conditions (ASC), have a preference for visual methods, strong avoidance of eye contact and benefit from very careful advance structuring with clear preliminary information so that they are not confused when asked about their views (Beresford et al, 2004). They also have a tendency to interpret questions very literally and repetitively. In contrast, while children with ASC may prefer visual methods, deaf or hearing-impaired children may experience an inappropriate overuse of visual methods.

Disability-specific considerations often concern accessibility. For example, in 2009, the DCSF Tellus survey (see earlier) added versions of the online survey in alternative formats such as visual (BSL), audio (talking) and symbol (widget) with, more recently, plans for the possible use of screen readers and other assistive technology. More generally, children with dyslexia often benefit, for legibility reasons, from text presented as black print on cream, rather than white, paper. These specialised formats and modifications enable the involvement of a wider group of children and so a more inclusive consultation or collaboration.

Facilitators may be involved as intermediaries conveying, or translating, the views of those interviewed when the views of children with learning difficulties or sensory impairments are sought. For example, a facilitator may interpret Makaton signs for the researcher.

Ideally, facilitators should be chosen by the child (Clegg, 2004) and in close collaboration with those seeking the child's views. This enables views to be collected from children who might otherwise be excluded (see earlier concerning possible parental gatekeeping). However, the filter of the facilitator may unwittingly distort the views held. If they are used, then any related report needs to acknowledge how views were collected so that the reader/listener can make a judgement about whether the conduit for views may have distorted the evidence.

Findings from these methods

It is clear that disabled children (as do other children, see Stafford et al, 2003) want to have the chance to express their views and to do so in authentic ways. Interestingly, parents' and disabled children's views often differ, which underlines the need for consultations about children's provision to involve the children themselves. For example, children and parents may take very different views about the desirability of in-class support or the significance of transport difficulties to out-of-school clubs (Mason et al, 2008). Emphasis in the school context has been on increasing parental rights and involvement (a major concern of the Lamb Inquiry, see DCSF, 2009a). This had not been matched with increased and genuine child involvement. There is evidence that, on the contrary, disabled children's involvement in processes around SEN statements and annual reviews have tended to neglect authentic pupil voice (Ofsted, 2009). Yet there are examples of effective practice in this context (Harding and Atkinson, 2009).

Disabled children may live more constrained lives than do other children. More so than other children, they report wishing for independence and autonomy, often in the face of parents' and others' understandable wish to be protective (Connors and Stalker, 2003; Lewis et al, 2007). There is a need for more 'whole-community' involvement and buddy systems to support disabled children's moves towards independence.

Disabled children express a strong wish to join with friends in informal, unstructured situations. Specific activities may be organised (e.g. via extended schools, arts-based groups, sports or faith groups) because they attract particular funding whether through formal systems (e.g. education, health, social services) or the voluntary sector. Such provision is highly fragmented; a research review concerning opportunities for 'fun and friendship' out of school hours for disabled children found many one-off projects, but little coherence across the field (Mason et al, 2008). In addition to the lack of a coherent picture of informal contacts there is a gap in understanding and developments around disabled children's views in relation to the more general, unstructured 'hanging out' with friends.

Themes for 'next generation' voice

Those working with disabled children in the context of voice need to sustain a recursive and reflective approach. This operates across all paradigms and contexts. It is a guard against the muddying of purpose that subverts child voice into others' agendas. Reflectivity should also prompt clarity in context (a listening culture) and progress in methods, so that these become more authentic (the child is communicating a genuine view) and valid (we are correctly interpreting the child's message).

Reflectivity also alerts us to points at which a child's silence, rather than voice, may be appropriate. Adults' facilitation of voice includes accepting that in some situations certain children, including those who are disabled, may not wish to share their views. Ironically, respecting children's silence may be more challenging with disabled than with other children as 'non-communication' by disabled children may be more readily misinterpreted as reflecting a lack of communicative ability and hence lead to redoubled efforts to encourage communication. (The same point applies to children from minority ethnic groups.)

Selling support for the hearing of children's voice has become a vast and growing industry. Multifarious fund-raising and training events are being promoted (often by freelance agencies or individuals, many excellent and well-founded, but others more opportunistic) adding to the large cross-professional and multidisciplinary infrastructure around the facilitation of child voice. Within that context, it will be tempting (in a capitalist system) to identify specialist 'niche' markets (e.g. 'disabled children') requiring (so it is claimed) a more highly specialised, or more comprehensive, subset of materials and approaches. For example, new web-based and digital methods can seem very seductive while not actually giving more children an authentic voice (e.g. an e-survey is not intrinsically more inclusive or more valid than a paper version). Companies promoting such packages also operate outside the rigorous ethical context required by, for example, universities or major research funding bodies.

An overarching issue emerging from the plethora of work on disabled children and voice is the fragmentation of disabled children's voices. They tend to be sought within the remit of a particular project or with a specific narrow focus, perhaps reflecting funding constraints or service foci. This means that the more holistic understanding of the child's views – along with inevitable fluidities and ambiguities – may be missed. Integrating those views into policy and provision requires a listening culture that permeates all children's services and experiences.

All children should have the chance to have their voices heard. The onus is on adults to find ways to facilitate this process. Methods for hearing disabled children's views are constrained more by researchers' and evaluators' imaginations than by children's capabilities. Limits to voice have been repeatedly overridden and a 'can do' approach will push boundaries further. However, in pushing out these boundaries the wider context of overlapping disadvantage and disability needs to be recognised. Checks need to be made so that the fostering of voice for disabled children is having an impact for all those children and not just a subset whose personal circumstances privilege their voices.

Notes

[1] 'Children' is used to cover children and young people.

[2] The term 'disabled' will be used in this chapter, for clarity and simplicity, to subsume 'disabled children' and 'children with special educational needs'/'children with additional support needs'/'children with additional learning needs'.

[3] Children as Partners Alliance (CAPA) conference participant, August 2002, Victoria, Canada.

[4] See: www.education.gov.uk/publications/standard/publicationdetail/page1/DCSF-RR218

[5] See: www.dcsf.gov.uk/research/programmeofresearch

References

Aitken, S. and Millar, S. (2004) *Listening to Children*, Glasgow: Sense Scotland/CALL Centre & Scottish Executive Education Department.

Alderson, P. and Morrow, G. (2004) *Ethics, Social Research and Consulting with Children and Young People*, London: Barnardo's.

Beresford, B., Tozer, R., Rabiee, P. and Sloper, P. (2004) 'Developing an Approach to Involving Children with Autistic Spectrum Disorders in a Social Care Research Project', *British Journal of Learning Disabilities*, vol 32, pp 180–5.

Beresford B., Rabiee P. and Sloper P. (2007) *Priorities and Perceptions of Disabled Children and Young People and their Parents Regarding Outcomes from Support Services*, York: Social Policy Research Unit, University of York.

Berlins, M. (2008) 'Junior Courts and Councils are a Bad Idea – Having the Maturity to Make Decisions is not Child's Play', *The Guardian*, 7 May.

Booth, W. (1998) 'Doing Research with Lonely People', *British Journal of Learning Disabilities*, vol 26, pp 132–6.

Byers, R., Davies, J., Fergusson, A. and Marvin, C. (2008) *What about Us? Promoting Emotional Well-Being for Young People with Learning Disabilities in Inclusive Schools and Colleges: Project Report*, Cambridge/London: University of Cambridge Faculty of Education/Foundation for People with Learning Disabilities.

Cameron, L. and Murphy, J. (2007) 'Obtaining Consent to Participate in Research: The Issues Involved in Including People with a Range of Learning and Communication Disabilities', *British Journal of Learning Disabilities*, vol 35, pp 113–20.

Clegg, J. (2004) 'Practice in Focus: A Hermeneutic Approach to Research Ethics', *British Journal of Learning Disabilities*, vol 32, pp 186–90.

Cocks, A. (2008) 'Researching the Lives of Disabled Children: The Process of Participant Observation in Seeking Inclusivity', *Qualitative Social Work*, vol 7, pp 163–80.

Connolly, A. (2008) 'Challenges of Generating Qualitative Data with Socially Excluded Young People', *International Journal of Social Research Methodology*, vol 11, pp 201–14.

Connors, C. and Stalker, K. (2003) *The Views and Experiences of Disabled Children and Their Siblings: A Positive Outlook*, London: Jessica Kingsley.

Crozier, J. and 'Tracey' (2000) 'Falling Out of School: A Young Woman's Reflections on Her Chequered Experience of Schooling', in A. Lewis and G. Lindsay (eds) *Researching Children's Perspectives*, Buckingham: Open University Press, pp 173–86.

Davis, J., Watson, N. and Cunningham-Burley, S. (2000) 'Learning the Lives of Disabled Children: A Reflexive Experience', in P. Christiansen and A. James (eds) *Researching Childhood: Perspectives and Practices*, London: Falmer Press, pp 201–24.

DCSF (Department for Children, Schools and Families) (2009a) *Parental Confidence in the SEN System. Final Report of the Lamb Inquiry*. Available at: www.dcsf.gov.uk/lambinquiry

DCSF (2009b) *Children with Special Educational Needs 2009: An Analysis*, DCSF-00949-2009. Available at: www.dcsf.gov.uk/rsgateway/DB/STA/t000851/index.shtml

Emerson, E. and Hatton, C. (2007) 'Contribution of Socioeconomic Position to Health Inequalities of British Children and Adolescents with Intellectual Disabilities', *American Journal of Mental Retardation*, vol 112, pp 40–50.

Fielding, M. (2004) 'Transformative Approaches to Student Voice: Theoretical Underpinnings, Recalcitrant Realities', *British Educational Research Journal*, vol 30, pp 295–311.

Franklin, A. and Sloper, P. (2009) 'Supporting the Participation of Disabled Children and Young People in Decision-Making', *Children & Society*, vol 23, pp 3–15.

Gray, P. (2002) *Disability Discrimination in Education: A Review of the Literature on Discrimination across the 0–19 Age Range, Undertaken on Behalf of the Disability Rights Commission*, London: Disability Rights Commission.

Grover, S. (2004) 'Why Won't They Listen to Us? On Giving Power and Voice to Children Participating in Social Research', *Childhood*, vol 11, pp 81–93.

Harding, E. and Atkinson, C. (2009) 'How EPs Record the Voice of the Child', *Educational Psychology in Practice*, vol 25, pp 125–37.

Hart, R. (1992) *Children's Participation: From Tokenism to Citizenship*, Florence: International Child Development Centre, UNICEF.

Hurley, J.C. and Underwood, M.K. (2002) 'Children's Understanding of Their Research Rights Before and after Debriefing: Informed Assent, Confidentiality and Stopping Participation', *Child Development*, vol 73, pp 132–43.

Kirby, P., Lanyon, C., Cronin, K. and Sinclair, R. (2003) *Building a Culture of Participation: Involving Children and Young People in Policy, Service Planning, Delivery and Evaluation – Handbook*, London: Department for Education and Skills.

Komulainen, S. (2007) 'The Ambiguity of the Child's "Voice" in Social Research', *Childhood*, vol 14, pp 11–28.

Lacey, P. (forthcoming). For background, see Lacey, P. (2009) 'Research: Update on the Inclusive Libraries Project', *PMLD Link*, vol 21, p 35.

Lewis, A. (2010) 'Silence in the Context of Child "Voice"', *Children & Society*, vol 24, pp 14–23.

Lewis, A. and Porter, J. (2004) 'Interviewing Children and Young People with Learning Disabilities: Guidelines for Researchers and Multi-Professional Practice', *British Journal of Learning Disabilities*, vol 32, pp 191–7.

Lewis, A. and Porter, J. (2007) 'Research and Pupil Voice', in L. Florian (ed) *Handbook of Special Education*, London: Sage, pp 222–32.

Lewis, A., Parsons, S. and Robertson, C. (2007) *My School, My Family, My Life: Telling It Like It Is. A Study Drawing on the Experiences of Disabled Children, Young People and Their Families in Great Britain in 2006*, London: Disability Rights Commission/University of Birmingham, School of Education.

Lewis, A., Parsons, S., Robertson, C., Feiler, A., Tarlton, B., Watson, D., Byers, R., Davies, J., Fergusson, A. and Marvin, C. (2008) 'The Role and Working of Reference, or Advisory, Groups Involving Disabled People: Reviewing the Experiences and Implications of Three Contrasting Research Projects', *British Journal of Special Education*, vol 35, pp 78–84.

Marchant, R. and Jones, M. (2003) *Getting It Right: Involving Disabled Children in Assessment, Planning and Review Processes*, Brighton: Triangle.

Mason, P., Loveless, L., Lewis, A., Morris, K. and Clarke, H. (2008) *Opportunities for Fun and Friendship for Disabled Children and Young People: A Focused Review of the Literature*, London: BBC Children in Need/University of Birmingham.

Masson, J. (2000) 'Researching Children's Perspectives: Legal Issues', in A. Lewis and G. Lindsay (eds) *Researching Children's Perspectives*, Buckingham: Open University Press, pp 34–45.

Morris, J. (2003) 'Including All Children: Finding out about the Experiences of Children with Communication and/or Cognitive Impairments', *Children and Society*, vol 17, pp 337–48.

Morrow, G. (2008) 'Ethical Dilemmas in Research with Children and Young People about their Social Environments', *Children's Geographies*, vol 6, pp 49–61.

Nind, M. (2009) *Conducting Qualitative Research with People with Learning, Communication and Other Disabilities: Methodological Challenges*, ESRC National Centre for Research Methods Review Paper, NCRM/012. Available at: http://eprints.soton.ac.uk/65065/

Ofsted (2009) *Annual Report of Her Majesty's Chief Inspector of Education, Children's Services and Skills 2008/9*, London: TSO.

Porter, J., Aspinall, A., Parsons, S., Simmonds, L., Wood, M., Culley, G. and Holroyd, A. (2005) 'Time to Listen', *Disability and Society*, vol 20, pp 575–85.

Potter, M. (2008) 'The Voice of the Child: Children's 'Rights' in Family Proceedings', Lionel Cohen Lecture, Israel, 4 May.

Roberts, H. (2000) 'Listening to Children: And Hearing Them', in P. Christiansen and A. James (eds) *Research with Children: Perspectives and Practices*, London: Routledge Falmer, pp 225–40.

Save the Children (2001) *Learning to Listen: Consulting Children and Young People with Disabilities*, London: London Development Team, Save the Children.

School Councils UK (2005) *School Councils for All: Including Disabled Pupils and Pupils with Special Educational Needs*, London: School Councils UK.

Scott, J.K., Wishart, J.G. and Bowyer, D.J. (2006) 'Do Current Consent and Confidentiality Requirements Impede or Enhance Research with Children with Learning Disabilities?', *Disability & Society*, vol 21, pp 273–87.

Sloper, P., Beresford, B. and Rabiee, P. (2009) 'Every Child Matters Outcomes: What Do They Mean for Disabled Children and Young People?', *Children & Society*, vol 23, pp 265–78.

Snelgrove, S. (2005) 'Bad, Mad and Sad: Developing a Methodology of Inclusion and a Pedagogy for Researching Students with Intellectual Disabilities', *International Journal of Inclusive Education*, vol 9, pp 313–29.

Stafford, A., Laybourn, A., Hill, M. and Walker, M. (2003) '"Having a Say": Children and Young People Talk about Consultation', *Children & Society*, vol 17, pp 361–73.

Stalker, K., Carpenter, J., Connors, C. and Phillips, R. (2004) 'Ethical Issues in Social Research: Difficulties Encountered Gaining Access to Children in Hospital for Research', *Child: Care, Health and Development*, vol 30, pp 377–83.

Stone, E. (2001) *Consulting with Disabled Children and Young People*, York: JRF.

Walmsley, J. (2005) 'What Matters to Vulnerable People? The Responsibility of Researchers', *Clinical Psychology*, vol 50, pp 20–4.

Watson, D., Tarleton, B. and Feiler, A. (2007) *I Want to Choose: A Resource Pack for Teachers and Other Professionals*, Bristol: Norah Fry Research Centre, University of Bristol.

Westcott, H.L. and Jones, D.P.H. (1999) 'Annotation: The Abuse of Disabled Children', *Journal of Child Psychology and Psychiatry*, vol 40, pp 497–506.

SIX

Building brighter futures for all our children: education, disability,[1] social policy and the family

Philippa Russell

Introduction

[We are] setting out an ambitious programme of action that will bring disabled people fully within the scope of the 'opportunity society'. By 2025, disabled people in Britain should have full opportunities and choices to improve their quality of life and to be respected and included as equal members of society. (Prime Minister's Strategy Unit, 2005)

Our aim is to make this the best place in the world for our children and young people to grow up.... Families are the bedrock of society and the place for nurturing happy, capable and resilient citizens. In our consultation, families made it clear that they would like better and more flexible information and support that reflect the real lives they lead. Our Expert Groups emphasised how important it is that parents are involved with all policy affecting children and that we need particularly to improve how Government and services involve all family members, including fathers. To achieve this, we must put parents' and carers' views at the heart of Government and find new ways of engaging parents as active citizens. (DCSF, 2007)

We recognise the importance of providing family support, particularly for those families who may be facing multiple problems. There will be a national campaign to support those families who face multiple problems, underpinned by local Community Budgets that provide pooled resources from 2011–12. Our key objective is to improve outcomes for all our children, recognising that some parents may need additional support in order to achieve that goal. (Ministerial contribution to debate on the Comprehensive Spending Review, 2010)

The past two decades have seen an unprecedented interest in, and development of, a wide range of initiatives around improving the life chances of disabled people (including the nation's children) and their families. Both the Labour and Coalition governments have stressed their commitment to support for family life as key to improving outcomes for the nation's children. The Disability Equality Duty applies to all public services and the principle of equal citizenship and valued roles for all disabled people has been widely accepted – if not always delivered in practice. New equalities legislation broadens protection from discrimination, and for the first time introduces the concept of 'associative disability discrimination', thereby protecting family carers and other citizens from discrimination because of their association with a disabled person. Outcomes for disabled people, like other citizens, are profoundly affected by the nature and level of their family support.

Families have also been changing and there is growing interest in the role of the modern family, not least in the interface between education and social care and support services, and the potential impact of demographic change in an ageing society together with changing expectations of women's roles and those for whom they provide care and support. The expansion and personalisation of social care services and the Labour government's 'Think Family' agenda recognise that families now need more personalised, responsive and flexible services. The Coalition government has reiterated the need to adopt a 'whole family' approach and is introducing an Early Intervention Fund in order to provide earlier support for vulnerable families. A recent Institute for Public Policy Research report (IPPR, 2009) also reminds us that many women now regard themselves as being part of a 'sandwich generation', where they may be providing care for grandchildren, children, disabled family members and older relatives in combination. As the National Carers' Strategy (DH, 2008) notes, a growing number of disabled people themselves are becoming family carers at a time when economic pressures are challenging the welcome shift to personal budgets, a stronger emphasis on co-production in managing the work–life balance and an emphasis on life chances rather than traditional patterns of care.

In particular, the concept of 'early intervention' has been expressed in a multiplicity of definitions at different life stages and sometimes with very varying intended outcomes. In the context of recent government reforms, in particular the 'Every Child Matters' agenda, earlier identification and intervention has been put firmly in the wider context of outcomes, that is, the improvement of all children's life chances. Every Child Matters set out five key outcomes as measures for the successful delivery of national policy across all public services, namely:

- Being and staying healthy.
- Enjoying and achieving.
- Being safe.
- Making a positive contribution.
- Economic well-being.

The same principles are reflected in the Labour government's aspirations for a more dynamic approach to social care, as set out in *Putting People First* (Local Government Association, ADASS and NHS, 2008) and the *National Carers' Strategy* (Department of Health, 2008).

The key principles within Every Child Matters have been embodied not only within national policy, but also within arrangements for local strategic planning and delivery. They also mark a distinct and positive policy trend away from reactive services (often delivered on the basis of deficit-driven assessments), and towards proactive policies designed to improve the life chances of the nation's citizens. The Prime Minister's Strategy Unit's (2005) visionary report, *Improving the Life Chances of Disabled People*, adopted a 20-year plan (Equality 2025, ODI [Office for Disability Issues]), with an emphasis on participation and citizenship rather than traditional care and protection. Similarly the government's Standing Commission on Carers will assist in the development of a 10-year strategy to improve the life chances of family carers, recognising the importance of valuing their individual aspirations as well as supporting their caring roles.

However, a major shift in policy towards improved participation and achievement by often underachieving and marginalised groups presents challenges. In the case of disabled children, a series of reports from the Every Disabled Child Matters campaign has highlighted increased expectations, but parallel concerns about equality and quality in access to services.

Historically, early identification and subsequent intervention or support have been regarded as services targeted on individual *children*.

From the 1970s, however, there has been a growing emphasis on *parents* as partners in any assessment or intervention programme and a parallel recognition that high-quality *family* support is an essential element within any early intervention programme.

The growth of interest in parents and families as 'change agents' for children with special educational and other special needs has led to an increase in a range of programmes that specifically engage parents as co-educators and key players both in the design and subsequent 'roll-out' of any interventions. As the Bercow Review (Bercow, 2008) promised:

> We must review the experiences of parents through the process of school and local authority assessment of their child's needs ... in order to identify how schools, local authorities and others can work better together to improve processes. Without the active understanding and engagement of parents, no intervention can succeed.

However, '*the active understanding and engagement of parents*' will not only necessitate positive approaches to partnership with individual families. It will also necessitate the use of early intervention through parent education or community programmes (such as Sure Start) to target disadvantaged families whose children may be 'at risk' primarily through a cluster of social deprivation and other general issues relating to income and lifestyle. In effect, improvement of outcomes for many *children* will depend upon *parent* education and support and a range of programmes focused on the whole family as well as the individual child. In the past decade, there has been a growing debate in the UK and elsewhere as to whether in some circumstances participation in such programmes should be compulsory.

As *The Children's Plan* (DCSF, 2007) noted:

> Our Expert Groups told us that the best way to achieve world class standards is a system in which all children receive teaching tailored to their needs and which is based on their 'stage not age'. This will require new approaches which adopt a long-term perspective in providing appropriate support for children and families at different points.

Both the Labour and Coalition governments' objectives to improve the life chances of *all* children through appropriate earlier intervention raise a number of challenges, not least when a child may require both specific targeted intervention right from the start (e.g. for multi-sensory impairment) and wider family support.

A changing population of children (and future citizens) with disabilities and SEN and implications for family support

New approaches to family-centred policy and practice must take account of a changing population of children (and a changing population of parents). In 2010, the population of disabled children looked very different to the population addressed by the 1989 Children Act and a succession of Education Acts.

Using the broad 1995 DDA definition of disability (which will include the majority of – though not all – children with identified SEN), it is estimated that there are around 11 million disabled adults and 770,000 disabled children in the UK (about 7% of the population aged 0–16). Since 1975, children 0–16 have formed the fastest-growing group of disabled people in the UK (from 476,000 in 1975 to 772,000 in 2002). This represents an increase of 62% (Prime Minister's Strategy Unit, 2005). There has also been a 60% increase in technology-dependent children since 2003 (DH/DES, 2004). The Nuffield Council on Bioethics Working Party on Decision-making in Neonatal Medicine (2006) underlines the long-term policy implications of improved survival rates of very premature infants, but the dearth of forward planning in addressing the high incidence of associated impairments and long-term health problems. The Council noted:

> The inconsistency of investing heavily in high-cost medical interventions to ensure survival and then discharging a growing population of children with major difficulties without an infrastructure to support them and their families in addressing often complex and long-term additional needs. (2006)

These 'new survivors' include children who have survived major trauma or illness with significant long-term health and other problems and also those children with specific and formerly life-shortening syndromes with improved survival rates into adult life. In effect there is a new and growing population of children with high individual support needs. The Council for Disabled Children (Carlin and Lenehan, 2006) has underlined the importance of families and the need for sufficient informed support not only for individual parents around the care of their child. but also for the full range of services that supports them (including early years provision and schools).

There has also been a significant (and unexplained) increase in the numbers of children diagnosed with an Autistic Spectrum Disorder or ADHD. Parents of children with behavioural disabilities now form the largest group of families seeking support from the Family Fund and these families are most likely to report problems in accessing both generic and specialist support.

Mental health has also risen up the professional and family agendas. In addition to a range of generic issues around protecting and promoting emotional well-being, Eric Emerson (2007) has noted the importance of co-morbidity in parents and children. He found that 33% of children with a learning disability had a mother with mental health needs. Children with a learning disability were also six times more likely to have a coexisting psychiatric disorder than other children in Britain.

'Behaviour' (however defined) has become a major concern for children's services in this and in other countries. The University of California (Robinson, 1999) found a 300% reported increase in prescriptions for children under five with behavioural difficulties or disabilities. A study by the Institute of Psychiatry (Scott et al, 2006) found that potentially severe behavioural difficulties were identifiable as early as age two or three, but appropriate early intervention and support for families were often not available. He noted that the costs of severely disruptive behaviour for these children could amount to £4,000–£6,000 a year and that two fifths of the children in the study were admitted to hospital for average stays of eight days in the previous year because of behaviour or accidents relating to their condition. He also found a high risk of depression or mental health problems in the mothers.

However, in looking at the changing patterns of childhood disability (and the reported rise of depression and mental health problems in parents as well as more complex conditions affecting children), it is important to consider the wider circumstances of the families concerned.

Money matters. Emerson and Hatton (2004), analysing the General Household Data with reference to the financial circumstances of families with disabled children, found that they were:

• 30% more likely to be single parents;
• 50% more likely to work part time, if working at all, and to be in debt;

- 50% more likely to live in substandard, temporary or overcrowded accommodation; and
- 50% less likely to be able to afford holidays, new clothes or 'treats'.

Current government policy rightly focuses on positive outcomes for all children, but currently there is evidence of lower educational attainment for disabled children. Of young disabled people aged 16–19, 60% are currently neither in education, training nor in employment (Youth Cohort Study, 2004, quoted in Prime Minister's Strategy Unit, 2005).

Improving the life chances of disabled children and their families – definitions of partnership

The past decade has seen a continuing interest in family-based practice in the best interests of children. As Dunst (2002) notes, such practice will necessitate treating families with dignity and respect; providing individualised and flexible services to meet identified needs; and seeing parent–professional partnerships as the bedrock of improving outcomes for individual children. However, uncertainties remain about how best to provide the resources and support necessary for families to respond to the challenge and raise children with confidence and in ways that meet the sometimes competing needs of children, parents and other family members.

In 2004, Sheila Wolfendale conceptualised parent–professional partnerships as the 'recognition of reciprocal expertise. Parents are experts on their own child, but – like any other expert – need information, advice and support in fulfilling this role'. At the same time, Michael Guralnick and the International Association for Early Intervention saw the importance of developing systems within which parent–professional partnerships could flourish, and defined the purpose of early intervention as:

> best conceptualised as a system designed to support family patterns of interaction that best promote children's development and optimise their access to, and use of, educational and other services which are usually provided for children in their community. (Guralnick, 2001)

Partnership is a key theme in all current government policy around children. The 2003 National Service Framework envisaged partnership with parents as integral to achieving all 10 standards and crucial in achieving the objective of Standard 8 (disabled children), namely an *ordinary life.* Definitions of an 'ordinary life', however, can be challenging for families caring for a child with a disability or special educational need. A parent giving evidence to the Parliamentary Hearings on Services for Disabled Children in 2006 commented that:

> "It would be lovely to be asked 'what would you like? What would make your family life 'normal'? Parents of disabled children don't ask for anything that other families don't get – it's just that when you have a disabled child, the structure isn't there, the system is not in place. You feel your views are not valued – and that means you feel that your child is not valued either." (Every Disabled Child Matters, 2006)

Some parents in the same report worried about the term 'partnership', one parent asking if it meant: 'Do it yourself, no help with all the additional tasks of caring, no recognition that you are just too tired to make use of anything without help'. Another parent, who had benefited from a 'Partners in policy-making' course (personal communication, 2008), stressed the importance of:

> "Building parents' views and preferences into the commissioning, the planning systems – and the need to remember that 'one size fits all' is wrong for families with disabled children. We are all different."

In the context of active partnership, the Parliamentary Hearings in 2006 received strong evidence of support for the role of the key worker (developed through the Early Support Programme) and the need for representation and advocacy for families when negotiating the system.

Both the Labour and Coalition governments' policy shift to personalisation of services for social (and in the future health) care through direct payments and individual budgets has been widely welcomed, albeit underlining the importance of proper information and advice for families. The Lamb Inquiry report (DCSF, 2009) reflects that personalisation in *education*:

> could provide an alternative to the current SEN Framework. With everything personally tailored, the argument is that there should be no need for a separate SEN system. It is entirely desirable that children should learn, progress well and achieve good outcomes with support from the mainstream of educational support.

The Lamb Inquiry concluded that the thrust of recent developments in personalisation (i.e. making appropriate individual responses through universal services) would strengthen the importance of early intervention and energise the mainstream sector, and, importantly, could be strengthened by the introduction of the Pupil and Parent Guarantees through the 2010 Children, Schools and Families Act. The Coalition government will introduce new legislation around support for children with SEN or disabilities, and a Green Paper, *Support and Aspiration – A New Approach to Special Educational Needs and Disability – A Consultation* (DFE, 2011), was published in March 2011. Like the previous administration there will be a strong emphasis on parental roles in improving outcomes for all children.

Family-focused interventions – the national policy context

A key factor in ensuring that disabled children and young people have better outcomes is that their additional support needs are recognised and addressed promptly and effectively. Many families will need additional support when seeking help for their children from professionals across a range of services.

A focus on outcomes as opposed to the process is a key theme across all government policy at the present time. The Prime Minister's Strategy Unit (2005) report, *Improving the Life Chances of Disabled People*, emphasises the importance of refocusing services and support on broader life chances and longer-term positive outcomes. Hendriks (2001), in a major Dutch study, criticises the narrow focus of many early intervention programmes upon outcomes for the *child*. These, he states, can no longer be regarded as a sole criterion for the efficacy of early intervention. *Family* satisfaction and competence are equally important 'markers' for the longer-term development of the child.

Parents as partners is a key theme within all UK programmes around early intervention. Parents are central to the objectives of Sure Start and within the Early Support Pilot Programmes (where the introduction of the Family Service Plan and the development of the role of key workers are seen as key developments to facilitate and support parent–professional partnerships). However, the concept of 'partnership with parents' has become more complex, as the range of options for early intervention has increased.

The United Kingdom has a strong and well-established voluntary or 'third' sector, with a wide range of parent support groups at local level as well as national organisations with local 'franchises'. Over the past decade, there has been a marked move towards engaging parents as 'partners in policymaking' as well as active players in the development and education of their child. Many parents, with access to the internet, are both more critical and aspirational with regard to their preferred programme or additional support for their child. The role of Parent Partnership Services has widened from individual support to engagement in local practice development. There are now Parent Forums in every local authority, many bridging the challenging transition gap between children's and adults' services and supporting families of young adult children up to the age of 25. The greater engagement of families in policy development also raises new challenges, for example, around the balance of inclusion versus specialist provision and the delivery of particular educational or therapeutic approaches.

In the UK, as elsewhere, there is an ongoing debate about determining the efficacy and 'best value' of different approaches to early intervention and education. As the National Autistic Society (personal communication, 2005) comments:

> There is currently a wide range of different options for pre-school intervention; parents will make their own choices according to preference, finances and time available. However, we urgently need a clearer evidence base for all options so that parents, education and other services can make the best possible choices at the earliest possible time and fully understand the implications of all options.

There is growing awareness of a range of issues around equality of opportunity for young disabled children and their families, in addition to access to services. The public sector duty to promote equality of opportunity within the 2005 Disability Discrimination Act will challenge many services to demonstrate equality and quality in terms of their ability to include disabled children. The recent verdict of the European High Court in 2008 on 'associative disability discrimination' (i.e. the right of a carer of a disabled child to bring a case of disability discrimination on grounds of discrimination because of their association with the disabled child) will also have implications for children's services and their attitudes towards the needs of parents or other family carers in addition to the needs of the individual child.

Parenting matters – creating resilient families and resilient children

In the approach to any general election, parenting and resilient families tend to go up the national policy agenda. In a recent national survey by Contact a Family (2009), 615 families of disabled children were asked 'What makes you stronger?'. The survey found a range of social, emotional and practical experiences in raising a child with a disability. As one parent commented, having read the survey report: 'It's hard. We (as parents) are strong because we understand that our daughter is not disabled by her condition but by the attitudes, policies and the surrounding environment'(personal communication).

Almost 70% of families said that understanding and acceptance of disability from their community or society was poor or unsatisfactory. Over 60% of parents still felt that they were neither really listened to nor valued by professionals and that society did not value or respect their role as carers. Over 70% felt that their child's access to play and leisure was poor or unsatisfactory and almost 60% of families reported the absence of key vital services such as key workers, short breaks and childcare. However, parents had clear priorities in terms of strengthening their role as confident parents. These included:

- more opportunities for play and leisure as keys to community inclusion, with real choice about activities and accessibility;
- seeing their disabled child achieve his or her full potential; and
- a support package specifically tailored to meet the child's *and* the family's individual needs and flexible and regular short breaks.

For many families, information on all available options is an ongoing challenge. As the Lamb Inquiry report (DCSF, 2009) notes:

> The survey carried out for the Inquiry identified the need
> for face-to-face meetings and for a range of information for
> parents. Overall, it identified the need for a more consumer
> focused and more personalised approach to the provision
> of information.

The Lamb Inquiry and an earlier report from the RNID (Gillinson and Green, 2007) underlined the importance of providing information – for parents and for disabled children and young people – in different formats and at different times. The Inquiry's survey replicated the findings of Contact a Family, and stressed the role of the professional as information manager and as the means of identifying and addressing changing needs. The introduction of the 'core offer' in the *Aiming High for Disabled Children* (DCSF and HM Treasury, 2007) programme offers new opportunities and, as the Lamb Inquiry notes, the concept of a 'core offer' creates a major cultural shift in the way in which parents' and disabled children's needs and aspirations are assessed and met: 'It shifts responsibility: it means that parents can expect to be provided with relevant information rather than having to find it out for themselves'.

Parents of disabled children are ambitious for change. Increasingly families with disabled children and 'disability activists' see each other as allies in promoting a more inclusive culture across communities, schools and in terms of careers and achievement in adult life. However, parents' ambitions are often achieved at a cost. The Lamb Inquiry report cites the parent of a young disabled man who has achieved well, had a good education and is now in employment. However, the parent also notes that these achievements have been at the cost of 'years of struggle and intensive promotion of his son's needs against a system that often did not seem to be on his side' (DCSF, 2009). As the father noted, he had only wanted his son to achieve his full potential and to have a normal family life.

As another parent commented:

> "If we were less tired, we would be able to deal with the social difficulties more easily. A tolerant and accepting society would help too. We talk about equality but our family feel the reverse!"

'The next generation' – listening to disabled children and young people

The past decade has seen a much greater emphasis on disabled children and young people as active partners in the design and development of services to support them. The inclusion agenda is strong, although variable in delivery, with a recognition not only of the importance of school experiences as the basis for a valued and skilled adult life, but also as a means of community engagement, friends and social networks. The Disability Rights Commission, in a national survey of the educational experiences and views of disabled pupils, parents and teachers (Lewis et al, 2004), found that disabled pupils first and foremost wanted schools that valued their potential; were ambitious about the future; and actively improved accessibility and inclusion in the whole life of the school. One pupil commented that:

"School matters. It's children's work, isn't it? If your school thinks you've got a future, that's great. The main thing is to feel part of everything. I'm on the School Council, I am helping the school to write it's Disability Access Plan. I'm also helping write their anti-bullying policy. Kids aren't always nice, it's horrid being called names. But we're managing it. I feel good, problem solving. It should stand me in good stead when I'm an adult – that's what I mean by inclusion, being listened to, dealing with things like everyone else!"

Another group of disabled children and young people, writing their election manifesto (Every Disabled Child Matters, 2009), similarly asked 'to be listened to and respected like anyone else – to be recognised as young people with a future'.

However, the Disability Rights Commission's study found that there was wide variation in the active engagement of disabled children in designing, reviewing and in some cases even acting as 'young inspectors' of services. The Commission concluded that 'the language of disability was often misunderstood' (Lewis et al, 2004), and, importantly, that many schools were anxious in talking about disability in a proactive way. Some young disabled people asked for adult disabled role models and one young African student commented that:

"Everyone wants to acknowledge my ethnic origin, to help me understand my African heritage and to meet people from my background. But they see inclusion as being apart from other disabled people. I want to be part of the community of disabled people as well as a member of my school on equal terms. We all need a peer group!" (Lewis et al, 2004)

However, she and her parents concluded that :

"We've made a lot of progress in helping disabled pupils to succeed. Inclusion is a big agenda, but really it's also an evolution. There's a lot to do, teacher training for a start, but there is a sea change in schools today. And disabled pupils are part of that change – our expectations have changed so much that inclusion is unstoppable!" (Lewis et al, 2004)

An agenda of change: challenges and opportunities in current government policy

Aiming High for Disabled Children: Better Support for Families (DCSF and HM Treasury, 2007), the Labour government's flagship programme for disabled children, marked the culmination of a number of reviews, recognising that: 'The long-term goal is to transform the lives of disabled children and to provide the ongoing support that they and their families need in order to fulfil their potential'.

Aiming High for Disabled Children set out local and national ambitions to improve the life chances of disabled children, offering:

- a new national indicator on disabled children as part of the new Public Service Agreement targets, to be agreed across government;
- a 'core offer' for families with disabled children;
- work to improve data collection (and hence commissioning) at local and national level; and
- a Transition Support Programme, recognising that the life expectancy (and therefore the life expectations) of disabled children have improved considerably in recent years and that disabled children (and family carers) have the right to a valued and purposeful adult life.

The concept of a 'core offer' reflects growing parental concern about the lack of transparency in determining eligibility for support services across all three statutory services and a recognition that access to appropriate support is subject to a significant 'postcode lottery'. The 'core offer' is currently a work in progress, but is likely to include:

- better information and advice;
- greater transparency (e.g. published eligibility criteria);
- active participation of parents and disabled children in assessment and decision-making;
- improved assessment (integrated across agencies and avoiding the current fragmentation and duplication of many assessment processes); and
- feedback, that is, regular communication with parents about procedures and outcomes.

Any introduction of a 'core offer' will necessitate major reviews of many statutory agency procedures – and hopefully improved take-up of existing positive practice in this area. In the Parliamentary Hearings (Every Disabled Child Matters, 2006), parents praised the Early Support

Programme's Family Service Plan and underlined the need for good information and communication strategies with families – and between agencies. As one professional giving evidence commented:

> "We live in an internet culture and it is no longer acceptable (or sensible) to let families suffer because of poor information and advice. We should also remember that we live in an age of litigation and unless we can ensure that parents (and disabled children) are active partners in the design and delivery of local services, we will have major problems. Information is needed at the micro and macro levels. The endorsement of individual budgets and direct payments as the way forward will personalise and open doors for many families. But it could conversely disadvantage families without the skills and resources to find the information which they need in order to be 'expert parents'." (Every Disabled Child Matters, 2006)

Aiming High (DCSF and HM Treasury, 2007) acknowledges the multiple practical challenges faced by parents of disabled children. Priorities identified by parents of disabled children mirror those identified by families of disabled *adults* in the deliberative events held to inform the 'National Carers Strategy' (Department of Health, 2008). Priorities included:

- Access to advice, information and advocacy (in effect for a key worker role).
- Short breaks (including emergency cover), which are positive experiences for families and recipients.
- Reliable childcare (or substitute care for adults) to enable carers to remain in the workforce. Although 85% of carers are of working age, 65% currently leave employment because of the lack of affordable and appropriate care.
- Greater transparency about eligibility criteria (and personalisation of services, with support for individual budgets and direct payments in principle – if adequately funded and backed by high-quality information and advice).
- Management of transitions (in the case of children, the move from children's to adults' services; in the case of adults, the transition between different levels of need and the carer's situation).
- Recognition and respect for family carers.

The Coalition government has also recognised the policy challenges and is making substantial investments in the provision of short breaks (for disabled children and for family carers of disabled adults).The emphasis is not on traditional 'respite', but more positively on high-quality inclusive breaks, which as far as possible enable the disabled children and older people to enjoy activities alongside their non-disabled peers. The personalisation agenda, endorsed by both governments, emphasises the importance of more creative (and more cost-effective) ways of supporting families and improving outcomes for children. A major transition planning programme will hopefully improve the consistency and quality of the move to adult life, described by many families as 'a black hole' or 'falling off a cliff'.

The Labour and Coalition governments' wider commitment to individual budgets and direct payments (already being piloted and evaluated for adults in a number of authorities) will be further extended through the first pilots for disabled children. This personalisation of services offers the potential for much greater satisfaction on the part of both families and children. It should encourage more flexible support, with an emphasis on individual choices and lifestyles. However, the shift to a more individualised service will be challenging.

A report from PricewaterhouseCoopers (2007) on the potential 'market' for services for disabled children noted the implications of moving to individual budgets without parallel stimulation of the market and frank and full discussions about the potential contribution of health and education to integrated individual budgets.The research team noted that moving to more individualised purchasing of provision would have major implications for local authorities in terms of stimulating the local marketplace and ensuring that a much wider range of providers were indeed 'fit for purpose'.

Most importantly PricewaterhouseCoopers note the need for high-quality information and advice for families as the new commissioners (and employers in some cases), and pointed to the role of the Centres for Independent Living (CILs) and User-Led Organisations (ULOs) in supporting the first introduction of direct payments for adults with physical impairments. In effect, they concluded, there were exciting opportunities, but also significant challenges in both creating a marketplace for a new and much wider range of services and supporting the role of local authorities and other public services in terms of workforce development, quality control and support for vulnerable service users. In making the new arrangements work, parents and carers would be critical partners – but would themselves need skills development and the capacity to work collectively in a broader policy context for the future.

To achieve a stronger engagement by parents in shaping local policy and practice development around services for disabled children, every local authority will now have a Parents Forum. For the first time, a new Public Service Agreement Indicator 54 was introduced, which is based on parents' assessment of the services that they have received. Although national indicators are being radically revised and reduced in number, the Coalition government's vision of greater community responsibility within the context of a 'Big Society' endorses the concept of Parent Forums and the wider engagement of families as active citizens in the design and development of local services.

Family care is not, of course, only carried out by parents. Young carers are prioritised within the *New Deal for Carers* (Department of Health, 2007), *The Children's Plan* (DCSF, 2007) and a *Memorandum of Understanding* (ADASS and ADCS, 2009) between the Local Government Association, the Association of Directors of Adult Social Care and Children's Services and the Department for Children, Schools and Families (DCSF) (now Department for Education), all of which note the level of stress experienced by young people who:

> Often feel [that their] caring role is vital and want to continue to help their families. But many young people tell us that they feel that they [are] missing out on their education and other opportunities and are isolated from their peers.

The DCSF's 'Think Family' initiative emphasises that services should adopt a whole-family approach and envisages plans for the new 'Family Pathfinders' as offering an opportunity to model a wide range of effective, preventative support around families affected by illness, disability or substance abuse, including those families who rely on the care of a child. Young carers do not see their roles as either negative or burdensome if they have the right support. However, as the National Carers' Strategy (DH, 2008) notes, adults' and children's social care services do not necessarily work well together, and children with disabled parents may fear professional intervention as potentially removing the child because of safeguarding issues. However, the emergence of innovative local services and, in particular, young carer support groups illustrates the capacity of the third sector to act as a positive partner in providing non-stigmatising care and support. Most importantly, as Nick Clegg stressed in his speech at the launch of the

Children and Families Task Force, the Coalition government has made a strong commitment to valuing families, proposing family policies that are fit for the 21st century and designed to enable families to flourish.

This policy will recognise that families themselves have changed and must include lone parents and step-families, and acknowledge the growing engagement of grandparents in bringing up children. More families are now providing intergenerational care (often including older relatives) and the role of fathers has changed significantly. Most importantly, disabled children and young people themselves are now seen as active family members with views and contributions of their own.

Looking to the future – a 'new relationship between parents, pupils and schools'

The Children's Plan (DCSF, 2007) offers a long-term vision of universal services within a preventative system. It envisages a strategic leadership role for public services, but with greater flexibility of providers. Children's Trusts piloted the concept of joint working (and in some cases joint commissioning and pooled budgets). The Labour government also envisaged new partnerships to build capacity and to sharpen accountability. It envisages 0–7 and 14–19 Partnerships and presents a vision of the '21st-century school' as having both a distinctive contribution (as now) in excellent teaching and learning and ensuring that children achieve, but also acting as:

> A vital community resource … it actively contributes to all
> aspects of a child's life – health and well-being, safety and
> developing the wider experiences and skills that characterise
> a good childhood and set a young person up for success as
> an adult … the school actively engages and listens to parents
> and pupils, makes sure their views shape school policies and
> works with them as equal and respected partners in their
> child's learning and development.

In effect schools have a crucial role as the hub of their local communities – but, for some, a real and dynamic partnership with parents (and pupils) will be challenging. The Labour government proposed a new relationship between parents and schools, with every child having a personal tutor; Parent Councils to raise the profile of parents in schools; and the creation of the new role of parent advisers to encourage traditionally disengaged parents to play a more proactive role in their child's education. The Coalition government similarly emphasises the importance of improved outcomes in education, with parents taking greater responsibility and also having more rights, for instance, in the creation of 'Free Schools' if they are dissatisfied with local provision.

The focus on parents is welcome, but it also raises issues about support for schools as well as parents (and pupils) in the new concordat. Parent Partnership Services and the new Parent Forums in each local authority should have a more strategic role to play (including development partnerships with the new Family Pathways and addressing together the long-term challenge of engaging 'hard-to-reach' families not only as co-educators of their child, but also as active 'partners in policymaking'. However, as the Lamb Inquiry notes, achieving real communication between parents, their disabled children and service providers will be an ongoing challenge. The UK has seen many positive developments in recent years, not least the emergence of the voices of disabled people (of all ages) as change agents.

The Disability Rights Commission (Lewis et al, 2004) found that 79% of parents (and young people) felt that their disabled children's teachers encouraged them to 'aim high' and 80% of parents felt that that the DDA has improved how schools and other services treat disabled children. The disabled young people themselves were ambitious, wanting a job, relationships and maximum independence in adult life. But parents also acknowledged that it was often the dreaded individual 'parent power' that brought results. One parent described her regret that she was seen as a "pushy parent, unrealistic, wanting too much" when all she wanted was "the chance for my son to have a life".[2] Her son, separately, admired his mother's tenacity, but regretted his dependence on her:

> "I'm scared about the time when Mum's not there. I'd like
> an advocate, someone to speak up for me apart from Mum
> and the dog! I want a career not a placement, work not a
> day centre. I think we are wasting talent here!"[2]

Conclusion

The Labour government's *The Children's Plan* (DCSF, 2007) offered an ambitious and long-term strategy for improving the coherence and quality of all children's and family services. For families of disabled children and children with SEN, there was a welcome strong policy imperative that local authorities should play a central role in improving outcomes for all children, through:

- developing sustainable relationships both in the communities they serve and between relevant professionals and providers and families;
- valuing families and creating proactive partnerships with parents in improving outcomes for their children, with an emphasis on self-directed care;
- commissioning services around the child (whether through targeted support such as CAMHS [Child and Adolescent Mental Health Services] or SEN or through school places, extended schools, etc);
- intervening when services are not delivered appropriately; and
- decommissioning inadequate services.

The Children's Plan (DCSF, 2007) recognised major challenges for families at key transition points – such as the Early Years Foundation Stage and the 14–19 reforms. It also promised personalised teaching and learning approaches for the 20% of children with SEN, with a strong emphasis on improving the workforce's knowledge and skills and understanding of SEN and disability.

Good health matters for all children and their families. Standard 8 of the National Service Framework for Children, Young People and Maternity Services (DH/DfES, 2004) set out an ambitious agenda for ensuring that disabled children had healthy and 'ordinary' lives. The Kennedy Report (2010) underlined the complexities of ensuring high quality health and well-being services for children with disabilities or complex health needs. The Coalition government in turn proposes major policy changes within the 'liberation' of a more patient-focused NHS (DH, 2010) and the shift to GP consortia and commissioning. The new proposals envisage a wider public health agenda, with the creation of new Directors of Public Health and Health and Wellbeing Boards to improve the general physical and mental health of local communities.

Joint Strategic Needs Assessments should encourage better integration of health, education and social care, and the Green Paper on new approaches to SEN and disability (DFE, 2011) proposes Education, Health and Care Plans to replace Statements of SEN and, it is hoped, end fragmentation of services and ensure better outcomes for children.

The personalisation agenda (for children and adults) unifies both governments' agendas, whether expressed more broadly through the concept of a 'Big Society' and greater freedom for dynamic voluntary sector and independent providers to transform the way in which services are designed and delivered, or through personal budgets and direct payments enabling families to enjoy more flexible and timely care and support.

The life chances of disabled children and adults are of course not only affected by the quality of 'traditional' children's services. The forthcoming welfare reform legislation will have major implications for families, carers and disabled people. Local authority budgets will be reduced and much more negotiation, advocacy and sometimes competition will be necessary between different strands of the community. However, families are high on the Coalition government's agenda, as are better outcomes for all pupils. If disabled children and young people with SEN are actively engaged in the debate about how we best support all our citizens in changing communities, then we can be optimistic.

Forthcoming legislation will determine the legal framework for the Coalition government's policy direction, but, now as in the future, there is an ongoing cross-party debate about how we can best end the cycle of disadvantage and lower achievement that characterises too many families where there are children with disabilities or special needs. The Green Paper *Support and Aspiration* (DFE, 2011) has set out the Coalition government's ambitions for disabled children and children with SEN. One message is very clear from both governments, namely, that citizen participation is crucial in the ongoing debate about tensions between big ambitions, the best way forward to achieve such ambitions and the management of radical change and reform in a very cold economic climate.

These are all ambitious policy developments – but they offer a real opportunity to address the historical fragmentation of support for disabled children and children with SEN and, importantly, they place rights and responsibilities (with appropriate support) on families. Importantly, they acknowledge the importance of personalised services and support, with an emphasis on co-production and valued lives rather than traditional 'respite' or 'care' services. Also, perhaps most challengingly (and most importantly), disabled children's and young people's own voices are being heard in the development of inclusive and high-quality national and local policy and practice.

Finally, as the Lamb Inquiry notes, we need to be bolder and more proactive in maximising the potential of existing legislation and policy requirements (in particular the rights-based disability equality duties that apply across education and social care) and to recognise that disabled children's life chances are profoundly affected not only by the quality of their education, but also by the support offered to families in order to lead 'ordinary lives'. As one parent commented (personal communication):

> The right to family life is a corner stone of Human Rights
> legislation. That means respecting the wishes, feelings and
> ambitions of children and their parents and supporting
> families as to be active advocates and valued partners in
> achieving good outcomes for their disabled children. This
> partnership is work in progress – but in the end it is the
> backbone of real inclusion.

Fairness, personalisation, co-production and a more responsive
and responsible 'Big Society' are key themes running through the
Comprehensive Spending Review (HM Treasury, 2010), the Coalition
Agreement and a range of recent government policy documents.
Beveridge noted in a personal contribution to one of the many
debates about the creation of the welfare state that radical change in
support for those individuals and families most in need could never
be easy. He was concerned that if citizens failed to see their potential
contribution to society, if they failed to value their health and well-
being, the nation as a whole would be poorer. He envisaged the greatest
challenge as determining how best to achieve greater equality. He saw
no instant solution, recognising that the achievement of true equality
of opportunity and well-being for all would be an ongoing debate and
a challenge for future directions.

We now not only have the major challenges of welfare and NHS
reform. We also have the challenges and opportunities set out in *Support
and Aspiration* (Department for Education, 2011), the Green Paper on
new approaches to SEN and disability. The Green Paper opens with
the ambition that:

> Our proposed reforms will respond to the frustrations
> of children and young people, their families and the
> professionals who work with the. We want to put in place
> a radically different system to support better life outcomes
> for young people; give parents confidence by giving them
> more control and transfer power to professionals on the
> front line and to local communities.

Many readers will welcome the broader refocusing on better life
outcomes, with a more transparent and less bureaucratic single
assessment process, better inter-agency planning and a strong emphasis
on parental choice, control and confidence that the system is on their
side. The Green Paper poses many challenges but it also offers a once-
in-a-generation opportunity to redesign and deliver the high quality

services and support which will indeed demonstrate that every disabled child matters (and every disabled child can achieve!).

Notes

[1] In using the term 'disability' throughout this chapter, the author is using the broad definition of disability within the 1995 and 2005 Disability Discrimination Acts (DDAs). The DDA definition also includes the majority of children and young people with identified and significant levels of special educational needs (SEN).

[2] Quote taken from personal communication from interviews the author conducted with families and young people as a member of the Disability Rights Commission advisory group.

References

ADASS (Association of Directors of Adult Social Services) and ADCS (Association of Directors of Children's Services) (2009) *Working Together to Support Young Carers: A Model Local Memorandum of Understanding between Statutory Directors for Children's Services and Adult Social Services*, London: ADASS.

Bercow, J. (2008) *Review of Children, Young People and Speech, Language and Communication*, London: DCSF.

Carlin, J. and Lenehan, C. (2006) *Including Me: Managing Complex Health Needs in Schools and Early years Settings*, London: Council for Disabled Children and National Children's Bureau Publications.

Contact a Family (2009) *What Makes My Family Stronger: A Report into What Makes Families with Disabled Children Stronger – Socially, Emotionally and Practically*, London: Contact a Family.

DCSF (Department for Children, Schools and Families) (2007) *The Children's Plan: Building Brighter Futures*, London: DCSF.

DCSF (2009) *The Lamb Inquiry: Special Educational Needs and Parental Confidence*, London: DCSF Publications Unit.

DCSF and HM Treasury (2007) *Aiming High for Disabled Children: Better Support for Families*, London: DCSF.

Department for Education (2011) *Support and Aspiration: A New Approach to Special Educational Needs and Disability: A Consultation*, Norwich: TSO.

DH (Department of Health) (2007) *New Deal for Carers*, London: DH.

DH (2008) *Carers at the Heart of 21st Century Families and Communities, the National Carers' Strategy*, London: DH.

DH (2010) *Liberating the NHS* (White Paper), London: DH.

DH/DfES (2004) *National Service Framework for Children, Young People and Maternity Services, Standard 8, Services for Disabled Children*, London: DH.

Dunst, C. (2002) 'Family-centred practices: birth through high school', *Journal of Special Education*, vol 38.

Emerson, E. (2007) *Family Functioning and Emotional Disorder*, Presentation on the Social Dimension of Mental Health, Lancaster: Institute for Health Research, University of Lancaster.

Emerson, E. and Hatton, C. (2004) *Analysis of the General Household Survey with Reference to the Circumstances of Families with a Disabled Child*, Lancaster: Institute for Health Research, University of Lancaster.

Every Disabled Child Matters (2006) *Report of the Parliamentary Hearings on Support for Disabled Children and their Families*, London: Every Disabled Child Matters at the Council for Disabled Children, National Children's Bureau.

Every Disabled Child Matters (2009) *Disabled Children's Manifesto for Change*. Available at www.ncb.org.uk/edcm/manifesto/downloads/dc_manifesto.pdf

Gillinson, S. and Green, H. (2007) *Beyond Bricks and Mortar*, London: RNID.

Guralnick, M. (2001) 'A Developmental Systems Model for Early Intervention', *Infants and Young Children*, vol 14, no 2, pp 1–18.

Hendriks, L. (2001) *Therapeutic Toddler Classes in Dutch Rehabilitation Centres*, Nijmwegen: University Press.

HM Treasury (2010) *Comprehensive Spending Review*, London: HM Treasury.

IPPR (2009) *Women, the 'Sandwich Generation' and the Modern Family: An IPPR Summary Paper Prepared for the Government's Equality Office*, London: IPPR Publications.

Kennedy, I. (2010) *Getting it Right for Children and Young People: Overcoming Cultural Barriers in the NHS so as to Meet their Needs: A Review by Professor Sir Ian Kennedy*, London: DH.

Lewis, A., Parsons, S. and Robertson, C. (2007) *My School, My Family, My Life: Telling It Like It Is*, Birmingham: Disability Rights Commission/University of Birmingham.

Local Government Association, ADASS and NHS (2008) *Putting People First: A Shared Vision and Commitment to the Transformation of Adult Social Care*, London: Department of Health.

Nuffield Council on Bioethics (2006) *Critical Care Decisions in Fetal and Neonatal Medicine: Ethical Issues*, London: Nuffield Foundation.

Office for Disability Issues (2008) *The Independent Living Review*, London: Department for Work and Pensions.

Pricewaterhousecoopers (2007) *Review of the Market for Disabled Children's Services*, Pricewaterhousecoopers.

Prime Minister's Strategy Unit (2005) *Improving the Life Chances of Disabled People*, London: Prime Minister's Strategy Unit/Cabinet Office.

Robison, L. (1999) 'National Trends in the Prevalence of Attention Deficit/Hyperactivity Disorder and the Prescribing of Methylphenidate among School Age Children 1990-1995', *Clinical Paediatrics*, vol 38, pp 209-17.

Scott, S., Knapp, M. and Romeo, R. (2006) 'The economic cost of severe antisocial behaviour in children and who pays for it', *British Journal of Psychiatry*, no 188.

Standing Commission on Carers (2009) *Report of the Standing Commission on Carers 2007–2009*, London: Department of Health.

Wolfendale, S. (2004) 'Parent–Professional Partnership', Paper presented at Council for Disabled Children conference, April 2004, London.

SEVEN

Access to higher education for disabled students: a policy success story?

Sheila Riddell and Elisabet Weedon

Introduction

Viewed through a lens of optimism, the position of disabled people in higher education has been transformed over a very short period of time. As recently as the 1990s, disabled people were largely excluded from higher education, and those who were successful in gaining a place were offered no guarantee of support. While legislation passed in the early 1980s placed an obligation on local authorities to identify and address children's special educational needs, it was not until the passage of the Special Educational Needs and Disability Act (SENDA) in 2001 that universities were placed under an obligation to avoid discrimination against disabled students by making reasonable adjustments and avoiding less favourable treatment. From this point, disabled students had rights to reasonable levels of support, rather than being dependent on the goodwill of staff and students, as had been the case in the past. However, as many disabled students discovered, gaining admission is only the first part of the challenge. Once admitted to a particular course at college or university, disabled students still have to engage in a daily struggle to access buildings, course materials and examinations. Building friendships and social capital, those invisible but vital elements of university experience, may also prove hugely challenging. Finally, coming to terms with one's identity as a disabled student, and incorporating this into a future identity as a working person, may also be highly problematic.

This chapter begins by outlining the progress made by disabled students in accessing higher education over the past two decades. Universities made very little provision for disabled students before the 1990s; since then, a range of policy and funding measures have been put in place (Fuller et al, 2009). Despite the evident gains, it is clear that disabled students continue to face a complex web of disadvantage. Whilst some issues, such as physical access, are relatively straightforward to address, others, such as the negotiation of identity as a disabled person in higher education, are much more difficult to tackle since they are regarded as private rather than public matters. This point is illustrated through the experiences of a student with a diagnosis of dyslexia, struggling with her own ambivalent views of disability and the discriminatory attitudes and practices she encounters on work placement. The chapter concludes with some reflections on the struggle ahead in the light of possible policy trends.

The research

This chapter draws on data from a research project funded by the UK Economic and Social Research Council as part of its Teaching and Learning Research Programme (RES-139-25-013) (for a further account of the research, see Fuller et al, 2009). The study, conducted between 2004 and 2007, was longitudinal and investigated the experiences and outcomes of a cohort of disabled students in four universities over a period of four years. Profiles of the four institutions were compiled, drawing on key informant data, statistical information and official documents. A questionnaire was administered to disabled students in each institution, and case studies of students were subsequently undertaken. The case studies involved interviews with students and their lecturers at intervals during their university career. The sample of case study students was selected in order to reflect the social profile of students within that particular institution. This chapter draws on some of the statistical analysis conducted as part of the project, as well as the analysis of student case studies.

The UK higher education environment

Over the past two decades, higher education in the UK has transformed from an elite to a mass system, with a significant reduction in per capita funding. At the same time, new public management has grown in influence, reflected in accountability regimes such as the Research Excellence Framework and Teaching Quality Assessment. Managerialist techniques have also been used to monitor quality in research and teaching, but also to promote equality. For example, universities are currently required to return information to the Higher Education Statistics Agency on the number of disabled students in specific categories, and premium funding is awarded on the basis of the number of students claiming the Disabled Students' Allowance (DSA). From 2006, universities have also been required to produce disability equality schemes, establishing milestones and targets to chart institutional progress towards greater equality for disabled staff and students. Managerialist methods have thus been used to provide both sticks and carrots to the promotion of equality for disabled students. These require systems to be in place to distinguish between the disabled and non-disabled student populations, which are likely to have knock-on effects on students' construction of identity.

As noted earlier, universities' duties to avoid discriminatory practices were given a strong push forward by the passage of SENDA, implemented in 2002 as Part 4 of the 1995 Disability Discrimination Act (DDA). The legislation had far-reaching implications in terms of its requirement for reasonable adjustments to be made to the curriculum, pedagogy and assessment, but in order to claim their right to such an adjustment, an individual student had to be able to demonstrate that he or she had an impairment that was substantial and had a long-term impact.[1] Depending on the nature and cost of the required adjustment, students may be eligible for the DSA. Under the terms of the Act, a person is disabled if he or she has a physical or mental impairment that has a substantial and long-term adverse effect on their ability to perform normal day-to-day activities. A medical certificate is generally required to prove that a student has a particular impairment. Students are given the opportunity to disclose a disability when they first apply for admission to the institution or at a later point, since it is recognised that a student may become aware of an impairment, or may develop a condition for the first time, during their time at university. Drawing a binary divide between disabled and non-disabled students is thus incentivised at the level of the institution and the individual student.

The Browne (2010) review of higher education funding and student finance has major implications for all students, including those who are disabled. The review works on the assumption that the government will withdraw at least 80% of funding from higher education teaching, with no or minimal state subsidy for courses in the arts, humanities and social sciences. This massive reduction in state funding will result in a sharp hike in fees for most university courses, with universities free to charge as much as the market will bear above a 'soft cap' of £6,000. Students will not be expected to pay fees upfront, but will have to pay back their loans as soon as they are earning more than a specified amount. The burden of paying for higher education is thus shifted from the state to the individual student and their family. Although the findings of the review relate to England only, a similar review is taking place in Scotland. At the moment, it is unclear how the Browne review will impact on disabled students, and whether measures such as the DSA and premium funding will continue to exist in the future. It is highly likely that better-off disabled students will continue to access elite institutions, as they do at present, but poorer disabled students, particularly those with stigmatising labels, such as social, emotional and behavioural difficulties, will find it increasingly difficult to attain a university education. Clearly, there will be a need to examine how the new funding regime will impact on disabled students.

The profile of disabled students in higher education

As noted earlier, when students apply to study at UK universities, they are requested, but not required, to provide information on their disability status. The university application form includes nine categories of impairment of different orders; some are medical or quasi-medical categories (e.g. blind/partially sighted, dyslexia), while others relate to the type of support needed by the student (e.g. personal care support). The last three categories (unseen disability, multiple disabilities or other disability) are very broad. At the point of application, students simply self-select the category that they think best describes their condition, although, as indicated earlier, they are required to provide medical evidence if they wish to claim additional financial support through the DSA. Perhaps as a result of the financial incentive to disclose, the proportion of disabled students in UK higher education institutions over the past decade has almost doubled, and now stands at around 7% of the total student population.

The composition of the group has also changed, with a decrease in the proportion of students with sensory impairments and mobility difficulties and a considerable rise in the proportion of students disclosing dyslexia. In 1994/95, 15% of disabled students were known to be dyslexic; in 2004/05, the proportion had risen to about 50% and has continued to rise since. Over the same period of time, those in the category 'unseen disability' decreased considerably (see Table 1).[2] In 1999, the National Working Party on Dyslexia in Higher Education attributed these changes to earlier identification in the school population, support through the DSA and the increase in mature students through wider access policies, who may not have had their dyslexia detected at an earlier stage. As noted by Boxall et al (2004), students with learning difficulties (i.e. cognitive impairments) are still largely absent from higher education either as students or teachers. Their inclusion remains a challenge for the future.

As a result of the predominance of individuals with a diagnosis of dyslexia, disabled students overall are more likely to be male than female. Two thirds of school pupils identified as dyslexic are boys (Scottish Government, 2009) and students very commonly carry over their diagnosis from school to university.

Table 1: Categories of disability used by HESA (Higher Education Statistics Agency) and percentages of first-degree disabled undergraduates as a percentage of total numbers of disabled students 1994/95 and 2004/05

Type of disability	1994/95: First degree (in brackets full time only)	2004/05: First degree (in brackets full time only)
Dyslexia	15% (16%)	50% (54%)
Blind/partially sighted	4% (4%)	2.4% (2.4%)
Deaf/hard of hearing	6% (6%)	4% (3.7%)
Wheelchair/mobility difficulties	6% (4%)	2.8% (2.5%)
Personal care support	0.1% (0.2%)	0.1% (0.1%)
Mental health difficulties	2% (1.2%)	4.6% (4%)
An unseen disability	53% (57%)	17% (17%)
Multiple disabilities	5% (3.3%)	7.5% (4.8%)
Other disability	10% (9%)	10.5% (10%)
Autistic spectrum disorder	-	0.7% (0.8%)

Note: No entry for autistic spectrum disorder for 1994/95 as category was not in use at that time.

There are also important issues associated with the social class background of disabled students. As illustrated by Table 2, which draws on analysis conducted by Riddell et al (2005a), about 80% of students in pre-1992 universities are from middle-class backgrounds, and disabled students are slightly more likely to be middle class than their non-disabled counterparts. Middle-class students are also over-represented in post-1992 universities and non-university higher education institutions (HEIs), although social class differences are not quite so marked here.

By way of contrast, children with additional support needs (the term used in relation to the pupil population) are much more likely to live in areas of social deprivation (see Figure 1). As illustrated by Figure 2, the association between deprivation and additional support needs (ASN) is particularly marked in relation to certain categories, principally learning disability and social, emotional and behavioural difficulties, and these are also by far the largest categories.

Considering these findings in relation to the disabled population in higher education, it is clear that whilst the increase in participation

Table 2: First-year, full-time, UK domiciled undergraduates (Scotland and England) by disability, social class and type of institution, 2001

	Pre-1992			Post-1992			Non-university HEIs		
	No known disability	Known disability	All	No known disability	Known disability	All	No known disability	Known disability	All
n	67,713	2,816	70,529	40,691	2,273	42,964	15,850	1,046	16,896
Professional	21	22	21	11	13	11	10	13	11
Managerial/ Technical	47	48	47	41	41	41	43	47	43
Skilled, non-manual	12	12	12	15	15	15	15	15	15
Skilled, manual	12	12	12	20	17	19	19	15	19
Partly skilled	6	6	6	11	11	11	10	9	10
Unskilled	1	1	1	3	3	3	2	2	2

Note: Columns do not sum to 100 because of rounding errors.

Source: Riddell et al (2005a).

Figure 1: Percentage of children with additional support needs by deprivation category, Scotland, 2009

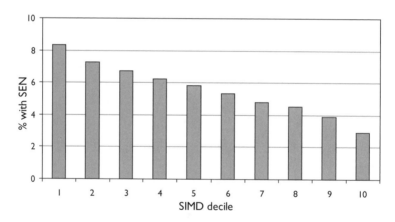

Notes: Children with ASN are those recorded as having a Record of Needs, Co-ordinated Support Plan and/or Individualised Educational Programme in maintained schools. Figures do not include grant-aided special pupils. Area with highest level of deprivation = 1, area with lowest level of deprivation = 10. SIMD = Scottish Index of Multiple Deprivation.

Source: Scottish Government unpublished data.

Figure 2: Percentage of children with particular reasons for support by deprivation category, Scotland, 2009, by SIMD decile

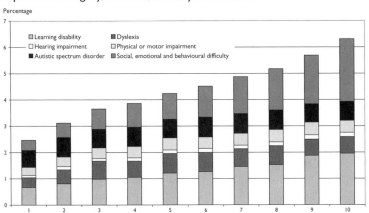

Notes: Area with highest level of deprivation = 1, area with lowest level of deprivation = 10. SIMD = Scottish Index of Multiple Deprivation. RFS = Reasons for Support. Some pupils are double counted if they have at least two different types of Reasons for Support. Grant-aided special school pupils are not included.

Source: Scottish Government unpublished data.

should be welcomed, warning notes should also be struck. Far from being typical of the disabled population, disabled students are a highly selected group, the majority being middle class, male and having a diagnosis of dyslexia. Disabled students from poorer backgrounds, who tend to attract socially stigmatised labels such as social, emotional and behavioural difficulties, are excluded from university study. Despite these social advantages, it is evident that disabled students are much more likely to be found in art and design courses, and are significantly under-represented in courses leading to the professions, such as medicine, dentistry and education. The application of fitness to practise standards by professional regulatory bodies may have a cooling out influence here (see later for further discussion). It is also the case that disabled people have much worse employment prospects than non-disabled people, with an employment rate of 50% as opposed to 80% for the non-disabled population (Riddell et al, 2005b). Exclusion from university is clearly one of the major factors contributing to this outcome.

Disability and identity

Initially, much activity in universities connected with the widening participation agenda focused on making buildings and estates more accessible. More tricky areas, such as the reform of teaching and assessment, have been tackled more slowly because in these domains the widening access agenda sometimes came into conflict with concerns about academic standards (Riddell and Weedon, 2006). Still less attention has been paid to how disabled students manage their identity both in the university and as they progress into the workplace, since this has been seen as a private matter relating to the individual, rather than a social policy concern. However, it is clear that the successful negotiation of identity as a disabled person has a bearing on future life chances, but may be extremely difficult, since the benefits of additional support may be outweighed by the problems of stigma, particularly when making the transition into the world of work.

It is now well recognised in social theory that individuals are not born with a fixed identity, but negotiate this with significant others over their life course (Beck, 1992; Lash and Urry, 1993). For example, an individual's age and parental status clearly change over time, and more subtle aspects of identity, such as social class, may alter as young adults move away from their family of origin. Other aspects of identity, such as gender, are unlikely to change, but at certain life stages may assume more or less importance. For example, a young woman discovering feminism for the first time may regard gender as the most important aspect of her identity, but at a later point in her life, ethnicity or social class may become more significant. Corker and Shakespeare (2002) have described disability as 'the ultimate post-modern category', since this is likely to alter radically over time and place. Disability increases greatly with age, and in all societies there is considerable variation with regard to what counts as impairment, particularly in areas such as mental health and learning disability. Despite the fluidity of disability as a category, administrative systems tend to assume that this is a fixed characteristic, and this may have both positive and negative consequences.

At least some of the increase in the number and proportion of disabled students in higher education may be explained by the fact that some individuals who were previously not formally identified as disabled now have this label attached to them. As noted earlier, students wishing to claim the DSA and receive reasonable adjustments in teaching, learning and assessment are required to disclose their disability to the university and to have this officially endorsed. However, the label may be accepted on purely pragmatic grounds, rather than becoming an internalised part of an individual's perception of self. This is particularly likely to be the case for individuals with non-normative rather than normative impairments, for instance, a person born with a significant visual or physical impairment may recognise disability as part of their identity from a very early age, whereas a young person who is diagnosed with dyslexia in school may carry this status with them into higher education, but may not regard this as a defining part of their identity. As students move into employment, the jeopardy of disclosing disability may increase, as a result of fear of discrimination. In the following section, we present a case study of a woman undertaking an Education degree in a Scottish university, whose status as a disabled student was helpful in the university context, but became extremely damaging on work placement.

Disability and fitness to practise standards in teaching

As noted earlier, while there are some pressures in developed societies to expand the category of disability to include socially disadvantaged individuals (Tomlinson, 1982, 1985, 1995; Stone, 1984), contrary pressures exist that lead people to reject such a label. In particular, disability may be associated with the idea of a 'spoiled identity' (Goffman, 1990; Watson, 2002), thus pressurising individuals to pass as non-disabled wherever possible. In the caring professions, this tradition is reflected in the imposition of fitness to practise standards, which were introduced with the specific purpose of barring unsuitable people from working in professions with high levels of contact with the public. For example, the Nursing and Midwifery Council, which regulates the nursing profession in England, Wales and Scotland, maintains that nurses must be of 'good health and good character' and operates fitness testing at the point of registration. Entry to teaching, medicine and social work is similarly controlled by regulatory bodies, although the standards are framed differently in the various professional arenas and applied differently in different jurisdictions of the UK.

The General Teaching Council for Scotland was established in 1965 to regulate the teaching profession, and fitness to practise standards were formalised in regulations introduced in 1993. Applicants for teacher training had to satisfy the medical practitioner for the particular institution that they were 'medically fit to teach'. Teaching in Scotland differs from the other caring professions in that, following a consultation in 2004, it was decided to remove the fitness to practise standards on the grounds that they were anachronistic and ineffective in identifying individuals who might pose a risk to children.[3] The consultation noted that the medical standards were initially introduced to protect children from infectious diseases such as tuberculosis, but such conditions are now quite rare and would only be detected in the later stages. Conditions such as HIV would only be detectable if laboratory tests were carried out, which were not part of the medical examination, and individuals with blood-borne viruses might well be asymptomatic. Psychiatric problems, it was noted, might also pose a threat to children, but there was no degree of certainty in relation to identifying which candidates might be dangerous. The General Teaching Council for Scotland published a General Code of Practice in 2002 and competency standards for full registration, which were deemed to supersede the requirement for separate health and fitness checks, particularly in light of the extension of the Disability Discrimination Act to cover the activities of professional regulatory bodies. By way of contrast, the Department for Education and Skills in England still insists that standards on physical and mental fitness to teach must be met by entrants to initial teacher training and qualified teachers.

In 2007, the Disability Rights Commission (DRC) undertook a Formal General Investigation into Fitness to Practise standards in teaching, nursing and social work and concluded that these discriminated against disabled people in the profession and led them to conceal their impairments or to leave their chosen profession early, as reflected in the very low numbers of disabled people in these fields. The DRC also argued that the standards acted as a deterrent to disabled people who were considering entry into the profession, and that occupational health tests applied by prospective employers might also deter disabled people from applying for teaching jobs, rather than being used to identify the reasonable adjustments that might be helpful, as required by the Disability Discrimination Act.

This perception is confirmed by data from the General Teaching Council for Scotland, which shows that, while disabled students make up about 3% of all students in Education, they account for a much smaller proportion of teachers on the Teacher Induction Scheme (the one-year school-based programme that all Education graduates

Table 3: Number and percentage of disabled and non-disabled teachers on the Teacher Induction Scheme in Scotland, 2002–06

Year	Disabled teachers	Non-disabled teachers
2002	12 (0.59%)	2009 (99.4%)
2003	6 (0.3%)	1808 (99.7%)
2004	16 (1.2%)	2018 (98.8%)
2005	24 (0.89%)	2670 (99.1%)
2006	31 (1.1%)	3509 (98.9%)

Source: General Teaching Council for Scotland.

undertake after their initial training). The number and percentage of teachers on the induction scheme is shown in Table 3.

The following case study that we present is of a student with a diagnosis of dyslexia on a BEd course at a time when the fitness standards were still operational (although these were abolished during the course of her four-year period of study). The experiences of students with hidden impairments are particularly important, since they represent by far the largest group of disabled students, and, precisely because of the invisibility of their condition, have to face dilemmas in relation to disclosure at many points in their personal and professional lives. The case study illustrates the individual's profound ambivalence in relation to the category, and the way in which the external environment is critical in terms of permitting or precluding disclosure.

Disability and the dilemma of disclosure: a student case study

Jean was a married mature student with three children who had decided to return to higher education to study a course that would allow her to find local employment. Her husband, a firefighter, worked shifts and was therefore available to help out with childcare. Jean struggled with spelling at primary and secondary school, but she was not diagnosed with dyslexia until she went for a medical, which at that time (2003) was a requirement for entry to the BEd degree. Noticing some spelling mistakes on Jean's form, the doctor suggested that she might have a dyslexic-type difficulty, which could be managed with reasonable adjustments on the course and in the workplace. Following appointments with the University Disability Office and an educational psychologist, dyslexia was formally diagnosed and the DSA awarded. However, the process was lengthy and support in the form of a laptop and software packages was not available until the second year of Jean's course.

Jean felt that there was a real stigma attached to having reading and writing difficulties:

> "I come from a generation where it was looked on very badly and you were regarded as being stupid and a dunce and things like that ... I didn't tell my mum for ages."

Although she welcomed the additional support she received at university, she found it difficult to see herself as a disabled person:

"I don't like the word ... not able, because of the 'dis'. I don't like it and I still don't know ... I still won't class myself as disabled."

Her image of a disabled person was someone with visible impairments, for example, a wheelchair user, even though she saw this as 'shocking' and 'awful' in the prejudices it revealed. However, being categorised as a disabled student did not sit easily with her overall sense of self:

"I still get emails from the Disability Office to register with [a disability group]. I kind of think 'I am not disabled'.... I mean there is one argument that labelling it might give you more resources and it has given me extra time which I am really pleased with ... but then I kind of think well, I don't know ... we all have strands and areas of development that can be worked on."

Despite the variability of practical and emotional support, Jean felt that her university experience had been largely positive and the adjustments made, in terms of extra time in exams and access to lecture notes in advance, were adequate. However, her experience of school placement was much more difficult. First, she had a difficult discussion with her Director of Studies (DoS) at the university about whether it was appropriate to disclose her disability to staff in school and what the consequences might be:

"I spoke to her [DoS] and she was a bit, like, 'Well you are going to have to explain to the school as it is, because when you do your probationer year it has to be disclosed'. So I was really shocked by that and felt very bruised that this was going to have to happen, and then she actually questioned whether I should be teaching in the first place. So I felt really, really bruised after that. She probably wasn't aware of, because I mean I still find I struggle with this, you know, it's the generation I come from.... So ... one of my good friends said to me 'Well I think you should just tell them and get the emotional stuff over and done with this year'. And I spoke to one of the tutors from last year and she gave me the same advice."

The reaction of the teacher in school, however, was extremely negative:

"I told the teacher at the end of my first week, beginning of my second, because I had got some major things done and I thought 'Well, she knows that I am a hard worker' … and her expression was, I will never forget, her expression was 'Really!'. And I just said to her 'Yes, you know I cope' and stuff and then the next day I went in and she was very close to another teacher in the school, and I felt like I had been discussed, and there was kind of looks being made and things, and then that teacher, from then onwards treated me like a child, and was very, very picky."

Jean received a diagnosis of dyslexia on entry to university, and, although finding it difficult to incorporate disability into her core identity, welcomed the additional support she received as a result of being identified as disabled. Whilst the university was able to make reasonable adjustments to teaching and assessment practices, problems arose in the context of work placement, where understanding of professional standards led teachers to question whether it was possible for a person with a diagnosis of dyslexia to be a successful teacher. Because of the negative attitudes encountered, Jean decided not to disclose her disability on future placements, nor when applying for her first teaching job. Given the very low proportion of teachers in Scottish schools who have disclosed a disability, it is evident that this scenario is played out frequently.

So what has been achieved – and what remains to be done?

We began by reviewing the progress made in relation to participation in higher education by disabled students. There is clearly much to celebrate, with disabled students making up more than 7% of the student population and entitlement to support underpinned by equality legislation. However, examining the figures in greater depth indicates underlying problems. The increase in participation is largely accounted for by the growing proportion of students with a diagnosis of dyslexia, while the proportion of students with sensory impairments and mobility difficulties has slightly declined. Students with learning difficulties have so far failed to gain access to the academy, and ensuring their meaningful involvement remains one of the great challenges for the future. Furthermore, disabled students, like other university students, are drawn disproportionately from middle-class backgrounds, whilst at school level pupils with additional support needs are much more likely to live in areas of deprivation and be diagnosed with a learning disability or social, emotional and behavioural difficulties. In addition, disabled students are much more likely to be studying subjects such as art and design, and are under-represented in vocational courses such as law, medicine, dentistry, education, social work and nursing.

With regard to the actions taken by universities to help students complete courses successfully, it is also evident that much progress has been made. The application of standards based on principles of universal access means that many buildings that were previously inaccessible are now open to all. At a slower pace, accessibility issues are being addressed in relation to the curriculum, pedagogy and assessment. Issues associated with disability and identity, on the other hand, have proved the most difficult to address. While many students are willing to accept being identified as disabled if this helps them access additional support, they are wary of carrying this identity forward into their working lives, where they fear stigma and discrimination. This goes some way to explain their low numbers on vocational courses, and their even lower representation amonge the workforce of many professions, including teaching.

In terms of the actions that are needed, it is clear that widening participation for disabled students is inextricably linked with other forms of inequality and under-representation in higher education, particularly in relation to social class. Often, programmes aimed at recruiting and supporting disabled students have been organised entirely separately from those aimed at socially disadvantaged students, and a much more concerted approach is required at the institutional level, which of course accords with the broad remit of the Equality and Human Rights Commission. In addition, while students are being actively encouraged to disclose a disability at university, they are being deterred from doing so in the workplace through discriminatory practices, including those reflected in fitness to practise standards. In line with the recommendations of the DRC review of fitness to practise standards, there is an urgent need to remove policies and practices that discourage entry to the professions by disabled people. Measures in the 2010 Equality Act restrict the circumstances in which employers may ask questions about health and disability prior to interview and should lead to a reduction in the screening out of disabled people. More careful monitoring of the situation would enable action to be taken to chart progress over time in the recruitment and retention of disabled people in the workforce, particularly at the professional level.

While inclusion policies for disabled people and others have been high on the political agenda for the past decade, there are concerns that in future these issues may be given less prominence. The present

Coalition government at Westminster appears to be placing much greater emphasis on the market as the arbiter of which students will gain access to which institutions, with a strong likelihood that inequalities in the funding and prestige of different institutions will intensify. In the new higher education marketplace, the place of widening access initiatives, including those aimed at disabled students, is unclear. At Holyrood, the Scottish National Party has stated clearly that economic growth must guide all investment decisions in higher education, and that social inclusion should not be pursued unless it contributes to this overarching goal. Finally, as mentioned earlier, there is a need for careful scrutiny of proposals for the future funding of higher education at Westminster and in the devolved administrations, in order to assess their impact on disabled students. Clearly, much energy will be needed to ensure that the gains of the last decade are not lost and further progress is made in making all social institutions and workplaces accessible to all, regardless of social background or disability status.

Notes

[1] Efforts have been made by the DRC (Disability Rights Commission) and the EHRC (Equality and Human Rights Commission) to change the definition of disability in the Equality Bill, so that an impairment would not need to have a 'substantial' or 'long-term' effect in order to qualify as a 'disability'. The government has not agreed to these suggested changes.

[2] Data from: www.hesa.ac.uk/index.php/content/category/2/32/141/

[3] The consultation is available at: www.scotland.gov.uk/consultations/education/medicallyfit.pdf

References

Beck, U. (1992) *The Risk Society*, London: Sage Publications.

Boxall, K., Carson, I. and Docherty, D. (2004) 'Room at the Academy? People with Learning Difficulties and Higher Education', *Disability and Society*, vol 19, no 2, pp 99–113.

Browne, J. (2010) *Securing a Sustainable Future for Higher Education: An Independent Review of Higher Education Funding and Student Finance*. Available at: www.independent.gov.uk/browne-report

Corker, M. and Shakespeare, T. (2002) *Embodying disability theory*, London: Continuum.

Fuller, M., Georgeson, J., Healey, M., Hurst, A., Kelly, K., Riddell, S., Roberts, H. and Weedon, E. (2009) *Improving Disabled Students' Learning in Higher Education: Experiences and Outcomes*, London: Routledge.

Goffman, E. (1990) *Stigma*, Harmondsworth: Penguin.

Lash, C. and Urry, J. (1993) *Economies of Signs and Space*, London: Sage Publications.

National Working Party on Dyslexia in Higher Education (1999) *Dyslexia in Higher Education: Policy, Provision and Practice*, Hull: University of Hull.

Riddell, S. and Weedon, E. (2006) 'What Counts as a Fair Assessment? Dyslexic Students and Fair Assessment', *International Studies in the Sociology of Education*, vol 16, no 1, pp 57–73.

Riddell, S., Tinklin, T. and Wilson, A. (2005a) *Disabled Students in Higher Education*, London: RoutledgeFalmer.

Riddell, S., Banks, P. and Tinklin, T. (2005b) *Disability and Employment in Scotland: A Review of the Evidence Base*, Edinburgh: Scottish Executive.

Scottish Government (2009) *Pupils in Scotland*, Edinburgh: Scottish Government.

Stone, D.A. (1984) *The Disabled State*, Basingstoke: Macmillan.

Tomlinson, S. (1982) *A Sociology of Special Education*, London: Routledge.

Tomlinson, S. (1985) 'The Expansion of Special Education', *Oxford Review of Education*, vol 11, no 2, pp 157–65.

Tomlinson, S. (1995) 'The Radical Structuralist View of Special Educational Needs and Disability: Unpopular Perspectives on Their Origins and Development', in T. Skrtic (ed) *Disability and Democracy: Reconstructing (Special) Education for Post-Modernity*, New York: Teachers' College Press.

Watson, N. (2002) '"Well, I Know This is Going to Sound Very Strange to You, but I Don't See Myself as a Disabled Person": Identity and Disability', *Disability & Society*, vol 17, no 5, pp 509–29.

EIGHT

Meeting the standard but failing the test: children and young people with sensory impairments

Olga Miller, Rory Cobb and Paul Simpson

Introduction

This chapter takes as its focus issues around the relationship between the assessment and attainment of those children and young people who have special educational needs (SEN) and/or disabilities arising from hearing, visual or multi-sensory impairments. In particular, the chapter examines some of the implications of a system of assessment in England that pulls in two opposing directions. This is exemplified in the framework of government policy put in place by the Labour administration through the Every Child Matters agenda (ECM), which stresses entitlement for all children and young people to universal services, against the thrust of other policies that push towards a system of setting and streaming based on ability, as determined by the outcome of a series of national tests and formal examinations.

One could argue that an approach based on setting and streaming is entirely appropriate in a society built around competition and that to argue otherwise is to undermine an education system that seeks to prepare young people for the stark realities of life in the 21st century. However, what is at the heart of any society is some form of engagement and participation. At a time of growing unemployment among young people in general and those with disabilities in particular, there is a danger that many young people will disappear from mainstream society and become lost in a growing underclass.

A number of these young people will not have thrived at school and may well have been assessed as having some form of SEN in combination with their disability and will certainly have had more than their fair share of difficulties. It is vital that the needs of these learners are understood by government before these young people give up all hope of ever gaining access to employment and lose the skills and independence needed to be successful. It is therefore especially important to identify those at risk as early as possible. To do this we need to know who they are, how many there are and what their needs are in order to plan appropriate forms of intervention.

Data on SEN

On the surface it seems a straightforward and uncontroversial suggestion that in order to match services to demand and need it is necessary to identify the number of individuals requiring these services. However, finding a methodology for collecting data in relation to sometimes contested forms of need is not so straightforward. Central government should be in an ideal position to do so, but despite the efforts of government statisticians, gathering robust and uncontested data in relation to pupils with SEN has proved elusive.

To a large extent the problem of identification of need has been compounded by an unclear relationship between the 1995 Disability Discrimination Act (DDA) (now mostly superseded by the 2010 Equality Act) and the 2001 Special Educational Needs and Disability Act (SENDA). Although the intention behind SENDA was to bring together the SEN framework with the DDA, in practice the reality has been very different. Understandably, schools and parents perceive the SEN assessment route as one that is familiar and firmly lodged in education. Disability legislation is often not something they are familiar with and may even be resisted by families who fear there is a stigma attached to the label of disability. In 2007, an Education and Skills Select Committee report (2007) explored the relationship between funding and the assessment of SEN with an acknowledgement that changes which separated the two aspects might be helpful. Indeed, the Apprenticeships, Skills, Children and Learning Act (ASCL), which received Royal Assent on 12 November 2009, should take forward this discussion.

Making a distinction between SEN and disability has also emerged as an area of interest for central government not only because it may help provide clearer data, but also because it may help provide data that incorporate more contextual information. It has become apparent from the problems attached to the current system of data collection that an alternative approach to the current system in England is needed.

In this chapter we appreciate that not all learners with sensory impairments would consider themselves to have SEN and conversely not all those with SEN would consider themselves to have a disability. However, we begin by using the term SEN rather than disability because the most recent data in relation to children comes from *Children with Special Educational Needs 2010: An Analysis* (DCSF, 2010). This statistical publication is published by the government in response to the 2008 Special Educational Needs (Information) Act. The data it contains are taken from the national pupil datasets, which are in turn compiled from the annual School Census.

These data are universally acknowledged to be less than robust because they define children according to broad categories of SEN, and in most cases only what is considered their primary SEN is taken into account. They also include only children in maintained schools who have a statement of SEN or are on School Action Plus. Added to this difficulty is that pupils' primary SEN is often determined by the provision the child or young person receives, sometimes without consulting specialist services. This means that the whole procedure can be something of a lottery dependent on the expertise of those completing the annual census returns.

For many years there was little attainment information about disabled students in the public domain. Sadly, the government's release of statistics related to their achievements in public examinations has raised more questions than it has answered. The collection of these figures is flawed – and the government itself raises caveats about their use.

Unfortunately, the School Census data are currently the only government data available, and if assessment of primary need is inaccurate or is not based on sufficient contextual information, the needs of some pupils may be underestimated or misunderstood. However, although the data produced by the government focuses on SEN, the term disability is often used interchangeably with the term SEN. This is an additional challenge for the government when trying to focus on improving the accuracy of statistical information, but is also problematic for those individuals who find themselves with a label of SEN or disability that they do not accept.

Nevertheless, the School Census data do highlight some important issues. The data indicate that the gap in attainment between those with and without SEN widened between 2005 and 2009, for 16-year-old pupils achieving the generally expected threshold of at least five GCSEs or equivalent at A* to C including English and Maths. The percentage of pupils with SEN who achieved this threshold increased from 8.0% in 2005 to 16.5% in 2009, an increase of 8.5 percentage points. However, the figure for pupils without SEN increased by 10.0 percentage points from 51.3% in 2005 to 61.3% in 2009.

Pupils without SEN also made more progress in terms of attainment between Key Stages 2 and 4 than those with SEN. Pupils with statements of SEN generally made more progress than those at School Action Plus.

In terms of attainment by primary type of special educational need, the data indicate that pupils with visual impairments were most likely to achieve the expected level at Key Stage 4.

Unpacking this data is not easy. Overall, it is clear that pupils with SEN do less well than those without. Considering that many of the SEN categories relate to learning or communication difficulties this is not surprising. However, the figures deserve closer analysis. As this chapter is written by specialists in visual and hearing impairment it is natural that we should take a particular interest in these disabilities.

Pupils with visual and hearing impairments

On the surface it would appear that pupils with visual and hearing impairments come out relatively well. As mentioned earlier, pupils with visual impairments achieve well at Key Stage 4 compared to other SEN groups – in 2009, 38.4% of those on School Action Plus and 27.6% of those with statements attained five or more A* to C GCSEs including English and Maths. The equivalent figures for pupils with hearing impairments were 36.8% of pupils on School Action Plus and 18.6% of those with statements. These figures compare with 13.3% and 6.1% for all pupils on School Action Plus or with statements, indicating that visual or hearing impairments are less of a barrier to attainment than many other types of SEN. On the other hand, the attainment of all pupils without SEN is 61.3%, around 25 to 30 percentage points higher than that achieved by pupils with visual and hearing impairments. It is more pertinent to explore the reasons for this gap than to celebrate the relative success of one disability group against another.

Vision and hearing impairment are considered to be low-incidence disabilities that are likely to contribute to a pupil's learning difficulties. Figures for 2010 point to 3.5% of pupils having their primary special educational need identified as arising from visual, hearing or multi-sensory impairments. However, this percentage does not take account of those pupils whose needs are complex and include sensory loss, but whose primary need may be entered in the School Census data as a severe learning difficulty or speech and language impairment. Nor does School Census take account of the fact that a pupil may have had a particular need assessed in early childhood and in the intervening years their original needs may have changed.

The Royal National Institute of Blind People (RNIB) commissioned research from the National Centre for Social Research (NatCen) on the educational attainment of pupils with visual impairments in the UK (Chanfreau and Cebulla, 2009), based on a more in-depth statistical analysis of the national pupil datasets for 2006/07. In particular, this analysis takes into account not just the nature of pupils' primary SEN, but also their additional needs, where these exist. It includes pupils whose secondary SEN is visual impairment as well as those for whom it is their primary SEN, so the analysis includes a larger group of pupils than that represented in the published Department for Children, Schools and Families (DCSF) data.

The RNIB data also includes other contextual data, such as ethnicity, gender, social disadvantage and type of educational provision, in order to judge whether once these other factors have been taken into account there is still a gap in attainment between pupils with visual impairments and pupils without SEN.

The characteristics of pupils are also explored in more detail in the RNIB study and as might be predicted those pupils with additional SEN in combination with a visual impairment consistently do less well and make less progress between Key Stage 3 and Key Stage 4 than predicted when compared with those pupils with a visual impairment and no other SEN. This finding is not surprising given the likely complexity and range of additional SEN.

Less explicable is that the research also indicates that pupils with a visual impairment and no additional SEN make consistent progress between Key Stage 3 and Key Stage 4, and that where there are performance gaps, this 'educational deficit' exists by the time pupils enter Key Stage 3. This finding runs counter to the received wisdom that inclusion works better at primary than secondary level and suggests the need for further research into the effectiveness of interventions early on in a child's education.

In the area of hearing impairment, similar attempts have been made to make sense of the published data. An article in the BATOD (British Association of Teachers of the Deaf) magazine in May 2009 (Powers, 2009) presented key information from the government data for 2005–07. This indicated that the percentage of children with hearing impairments achieving five or more A* to C GCSEs including English and Maths rose from 25% in 2005 to 27% in 2007, against a rise from 44% to 46% for all pupils. The absolute gap between all pupils and those with hearing impairments remained the same at 19 points, while the relative improvement was 8% for pupils with hearing impairments and 4.5% for all pupils.

While pointing out the positive trends shown by this data, Powers (2009) also highlights its limitations: 'For attainment data to be really useful we also need information on the key factors involved, not least degree of hearing loss, age at diagnosis and additional need'. The RNIB has identified similar issues from its research and plans to explore in more depth the range of contextual factors, both internal and external to the child, which might influence levels of attainment, such as the severity of sight loss. The NatCen study suggests that there are factors associated with the attainment of pupils with visual impairments, including those with additional SEN, which may not relate directly to their visual impairment at all. In common with other groups of pupils, these include living in an area of social deprivation and being eligible for Free School Meals. Other potential factors affecting pupils with both visual and hearing impairments could include the quality and extent of early intervention to reduce any negative impact of disability on the development of language, literacy and social interaction skills, which are considered to form the bedrock of future educational success.

Measuring attainment

The imperative to measure attainment and to demonstrate progress has reached new heights in the SEN and Learning Difficulties and Disabilities (LDD) *Progression Guidance* strategy (DCSF, 2009a) in what many teachers may see as the bizarre policy that pupils with SEN and severe (often profound) learning difficulties should be expected to make two levels of progress on the P-level scale[1] per year. On the one hand, this can be seen as an admirable commitment to ensuring that children with complex needs are fully included and not condemned by low expectations; while, on the other, it may appear to be shoehorning those with very individual needs into a system that rests on an assumption that the complexity of their attainment and progress can be described in simple numerical terms. This rather contentious policy could also be seen in terms of aspiration and naivety or more likely viewed with suspicion by teachers as a form of political manipulation.

Underlying much of this debate is the fundamental question of what we mean by educational attainment. The OECD Glossary of Statistical Terms defines it as 'the highest grade completed within the most advanced level attended in the educational system of the country where the education was received'.[2] Attainment is expressed in terms of educational qualifications, which are recognised as a key enabler for obtaining employment. The Strategy Unit's research report *Improving the Life Chances of Disabled People* (Cabinet Office, 2005) demonstrates that over 40% of disabled people suffer some form of labour-market disadvantage because they have no qualifications.

The national framework for assessment is set by government. Ofqual is the regulator, but the Qualifications and Curriculum Development Agency (QCDA), which used to provide advice, is to be abolished by the Coalition government and some of its functions will return to the Department for Education. Public examinations are designed by awarding bodies according to the specifications laid down by Ofqual and are subject to the provisions of the 1995 Disability Discrimination Act.

Educational attainment is measured through an assessment system that is firmly embedded in UK culture. This system depends largely on traditional pen and paper examinations, which are increasingly out of step with the technology that is so central to much of our work and leisure. There is a continuing belief that this approach acts as a leveller, placing all learners on the same footing and allowing them to be measured fairly against assessment objectives that are in some sense pure and universal. Yet in truth assessment only measures what we choose to think is important. As Stobart (2008, p 1) argues: 'Assessment does not objectively measure what is already there, but rather creates and shapes what is measured – it is capable of "making up people".'

Historically, assessment systems have been designed around the needs of the majority, with access arrangements subsequently 'bolted on' to take account of minorities, such as disabled candidates. Tensions are clearly apparent in current attempts to move from this medically based model of disability to a social model where the needs and skills of different groups are embraced from the outset through a process of universal or inclusive design.

On balance, it appears that our current understanding of attainment data for learners with SEN generates far more questions than answers. Certainly the data that are currently provided by central government are insufficient to make sense of what is going on. At one level it may seem obvious why children with SEN attain less well than those without, but what this may really be telling us is that we are measuring everyone with the same blunt instrument. This is the old formative versus summative argument, that knowing what a child has achieved is only meaningful if it helps you to understand the factors that led to this achievement. In addition, the complexity of the needs of many sensory impaired young people makes summative assessment significantly less informative than for their peers as it fails to recognise key factors influencing raw results in attainment and thus conceals their real attainment.

An example of this difficulty is the new information and communication technology (ICT) Functional Skills qualification, which forms a compulsory part of the new Diploma and Apprenticeship framework. 'Functional Skills are the fundamental applied skills in English, information and communication technology (ICT) and mathematics that help people to gain the most from life, learning and work' (Ofqual, 2009). ICT is a central tool in the lives of many blind and partially sighted learners, allowing them to access and manage information on equal terms with sighted people. It surely goes without saying that any test of functional ICT competence should build in an equal opportunity for visually impaired students to demonstrate their ICT skills and to do so on their own terms.

This is not the case, however. The standards for the new qualification include an automatic expectation that being competent in ICT means using a mouse and working with graphics, so there is every chance that a blind student will not be able to pass it. The fundamental problem here is an assumption that everybody's functional skills have to be the same. If you are blind, the things you are going to do with technology and the way you do them will not be the same as a sighted person, because they will be looking at the screen and you will not. Providing you with reasonable adjustments is not the answer if there is no recognition of the impact of your disability in the standards themselves. It is not a question of lower, but different expectations, which give credit for the many specialist ICT skills that a blind person may possess rather than penalising them for not being able to demonstrate those for which vision is essential.

This line of thought suggests that there may be instances where the concept of fully inclusive design may need to be refined by the development of alternative pathways to the same qualification, with a choice of units available to all candidates that provide a choice of tasks and working methods. The qualifications gained by disabled candidates would, therefore, be a more accurate reflection of their actual working methods, emphasising the importance of a policy of 'different but equal'. However, there is a danger that these alternative pathways might only be taken by disabled people, in which case qualifications including these units could be seen as less worthwhile than the 'standard' version. If so, this approach could end up reinforcing the difference between disabled and non-disabled people.

Arguably, therefore, anti-discrimination legislation has placed too much emphasis on equality rather than equity, with the result that disabled learners are always expected to achieve the same outcomes as their non-disabled peers even when it would sometimes make more sense to assess their skills in relation to outcomes that reflect the particular ways in which they learn and study. Additionally, as long as attainment is seen exclusively in terms of academic achievement it will never reflect the wider curriculum experience that schools are meant to be providing for their pupils under the ECM agenda. We might also question how effectively the access arrangements and reasonable adjustments discussed elsewhere in this chapter achieve their aim of removing disadvantage for learners with SEN and disability.

Are we effectively trying to fit square pegs into round holes? Here we need to make the point again that assessment is not an objective activity that exists above and outside the values of the society in which it takes place. Outside public examinations, classroom practice demonstrates a wide range of assessment processes. Assessment guidance is offered by government, including, recently, the concept of Assessment for Learning.

Defining assessment

The *Secretary of State Report on Progress towards Disability Equality across the Children's and Education Sector* (DCSF, 2008) declares that a wider range of assessment strategies should help identify and celebrate the full range of learners' achievements, and states that Assessment for Learning should be firmly embedded throughout schools.

A successful school uses 'assessment for learning – using data to track, monitor and respond to individual pupil progress, and ensuring that progress informs next steps' (DSCF, 2009b). Linked to this is Assessing Pupils' Progress (APP) – a structured approach to teacher assessment developed by the QCDA in partnership with the National Strategies, and its use is also encouraged as it 'helps teachers to fine-tune their understanding of pupils' needs and tailor their planning and teaching accordingly' (DCSF, 2009c).

The National Curriculum Inclusion Statement underlines the importance of the wider purposes of assessment and sets out the requirement for teachers to adapt the curriculum as necessary by 'setting suitable learning challenges, responding to pupils' diverse learning needs and overcoming potential barriers to learning and assessment for individuals and groups of pupils'.[3] This approach seems incompatible with that adopted in public examinations such as SATs and GCSEs where summative assessment is the key – indeed, coursework elements in GCSEs have recently been reduced or removed in many subjects in response to public concerns. Thus, unfounded public views have a direct influence on assessment policy, which in turn has a disproportionate effect on disabled students.

It is, of course, difficult to measure other more qualitative aspects of pupils' achievement such as those highlighted through the ECM publications (DfES, 2003), and to use them to form the basis for developing competition between schools. At present, performance is represented through what are characterised as 'league tables', which are seen by the government as providing information for parents and schools about the ranking of school success rates in terms of summative assessments. Consequently, examination results are given greater emphasis.

However, the previous government was aware of the problems inherent in relying too much on raw attainment results and intended to move to the collection of a limited number of wider measures, suggesting that 'we will develop a new School Report Card (SRC) for every school, which will provide a rounded assessment of school performance and enable parents and the public to make better informed judgments about the effectiveness of each school' (DCSF, 2009b). Even here, however, examination results would still be given prominence and a single grade for the school will emerge at the end allowing crude ranking to continue.

There is continuing pressure for further release of information including that related to disabled students and those with SEN. The view of the previous government was that low expectations prevail: 'for too long we have not set high enough ambitions for children with special educational needs' (DCSF, 2009c). This was echoed by Sarah Teather MP, Children's Minister for the Conservative–Liberal Democrat Coalition government, when launching the call for views on the SEN and Disability Green Paper: 'Children with special educational needs and disabilities should have the same opportunities as other children, but the current system is so adversarial that too often this doesn't happen.'[4]

The overarching approach to assessment in which disabled students are subsumed is influenced by notions of public accountability, which have recently assumed a more prominent position in the political world than ever before and are in danger of significantly overshadowing the formative purposes. In a letter to Lord Low (29 October 2009), Baroness Morgan (then Parliamentary Under-secretary of State for Children, Young People and Families) took up the issue around public confidence and qualifications in the following response:

> Although Ofqual's objective to secure public confidence in qualifications would ultimately be trumped by duties in the Equalities Bill, Ofqual will, of course, have to try to secure both. They will need to ensure that the qualifications system is accessible and that confidence in the system for all learners is maintained. That will not be easy, and Ofqual will not be able to do it alone.

Baroness Morgan went on to highlight the creation of advisory groups such as the 'Access Consultation Forum' where awarding bodies and disability groups come together to discuss these issues and advise Ofqual. The Equality Act 2010 (section 96) gave Ofqual the power to decide which aspects of qualifications should not be subject to reasonable adjustments. Ofqual has consulted with individual disability groups, held seminars, issued a consultation document and held public events at which these issues were discussed. At the time of writing the conclusions have not been reached but the process, indicating a strong and rigorous collaborative approach, has been encouraging.

Other related developments may also have potentially positive consequences. The revised Ofsted framework (Ofsted, 2009) states that the school's equality and diversity grade, which would include assessment and provision for children with SEN and disability, will be a limiting factor. Schools that achieve an 'inadequate' grade in this area will be unlikely to get more than satisfactory for their overall grade, with those achieving 'satisfactory' unlikely to achieve more than 'good' overall. This should herald a greater concentration in mainstream schools on the appropriate assessment of the needs of disabled students, although the Ofsted judgement will depend on the ability and understanding of the inspectors themselves.

Conclusion

Evidence from the US indicates that an undue emphasis on examination results and league tables has already had a negative effect on disabled children. For example, the requirements of the Individuals with Disabilities and Education Act (IDEA) in combination with the requirements of the No Child Left Behind (NCLB) legislation require that each state must demonstrate that it has developed and implemented a single state-wide accountability system and that the test results of schools must be published. Furthermore, for a school to prove it has made sufficient progress, each group of pupils must reach or exceed the targets set by the state as measures of progress. Of particular relevance to this chapter is the requirement that not less than 95% of each group of pupils on the school roll is required to take the assessments with appropriate accommodations or alternative assessments in line with the IDEA legislation.

There are significant penalties in place for schools whose pupils do not meet the required targets. One of these penalties is the option for pupils to be transferred to another public school. Clearly, therefore, it becomes in the best interests of a school to keep the number of pupils covered by NCLB to a minimum. Ironically, what was intended as a safeguard for disabled pupils may have proved a disincentive for schools to accept such pupils and evidence suggests that, for example, deaf children who have not done well in public schools are now being 'shifted to schools for the deaf' (Marschark, 2007).

The outcome of public examinations is growing in significance and the importance of qualifications for disabled people cannot be overestimated; especially in view of the high rates of unemployment among this group – far greater than the rates for non-disabled people. Reports by the Royal National Institute for Deaf People (RNID) show that the rate of unemployment for deaf people is four times greater than for hearing people, while research by the Network 1000 project into the lives of visually impaired adults found that only 34% of those registered as blind or partially sighted of working age were in employment, which compares with an overall employment rate of around 75% in 2007 (Douglas et al, 2009). Qualifications are essential in ensuring progression to suitable employment and higher education, for without skills and qualifications, today's young people will struggle to find meaningful work in the future. It is thus crucial that all barriers within examinations are removed.

As a response to the requirements of the 1995 DDA following its extension to general qualifications in 2007, government departments and several agencies are seriously endeavouring to address the issues of accessibility to examinations for disabled candidates. In its Single Equality Duty, the former government agency with responsibility for qualifications, the QCA, stated:

> This approach is applied through the equality impact assessment of QCA policies at the design stage, which allows us to see the potential barriers for disabled people early enough to remove or reduce them, so that the effect of the policy is not disadvantageous.

Many agencies have come to the view that the solution lies in the initial design of the qualifications, rather than relying entirely on post hoc adjustments such as the modification of carrier language or visual material in the original paper. In response to this, Ofqual has developed inclusion sheets, which are used to try to ensure that barriers are addressed and where possible removed at the point of qualification design. Awarding bodies and regulators have set up regular meetings – the Access Consultation Forum and Access to Assessment and Qualifications Advisory Group – at which they meet with professional associations and disability groups. Many issues raised by these groups have been addressed and this process of consultation is beginning to have a real influence on policy and practice. However, the continued existence of exemptions (where a section of a qualification is removed because it is inaccessible to some disabled students) raises concerns that truly inclusive qualifications will not be developed because an exemption can always be used as a last resort.

The accessibility of qualifications raises a number of issues. Governments of any political view are likely to be concerned not to appear to be watering down qualifications, and thus undermining public confidence in their integrity, by the application of reasonable adjustments. The 2010 Equality Act is a clear example of this, implying that reasonable adjustments for students are acceptable only as long as they do not undermine public confidence. The need for public education to ensure that the issues are understood and that accessibility for disabled candidates is not equated with 'dumbing down' by the public and employers is not mentioned.

Although there has been progress in many aspects of the provision of qualifications for disabled students, this chapter suggests that there is still a long way to go. It would be tragic if the system that should be designed to reward their achievements ultimately did no more than create additional barriers to their success.

Notes

[1] P scales are a set of descriptions for recording the achievement of pupils with SEN who are working towards level 1 of the National Curriculum.

[2] See the OECD website. Available at: http://stats.oecd.org/glossary/detail. asp?ID=742

[3] QCDA Inclusion Statement: http://curriculum.qcda.gov.uk/key-stages-3-and-4/About-the-secondary-curriculum/equalities-diversity-and-inclusion/including-all-learners/index.aspx

[4] Available at: www.education.gov.uk/childrenandyoungpeople/specialeducationalneeds/a0064387/childrens-minister-unveils-plans-for-education-of-sen-pupils

References

Cabinet Office (2005) *Improving the Life Chances of Disabled People*, London: The Stationery Office.

Chanfreau, J. and Cebulla, A. (2009) *Educational Attainment of Blind and Partially Sighted Pupils*, London: National Centre of Social Research (for RNIB).

DCSF (Department for Children, Schools and Families) (2008) *Secretary of State Report on Progress towards Disability Equality across the Children's and Education Sector*. Available at: www.dcsf.gov.uk/des/docs/2008Se cretaryofStateReport_a.pdf

DCSF (2009a) *Progression Guidance 2009–10 Improving Data to Raise Attainment and Maximise the Progress of Learners with Special Educational Needs, Learning Difficulties and Disabilities*, Nottingham: DCSF.

DCSF (2009b) *Your Child, Your Schools, Our Future: Building a 21st Century Schools System*, London: TSO.

DCSF (2009c) *National Strategies Progression Guidance 2009-2010*, London: DCSF.

DCSF (2010) *Children with Special Educational Needs 2010: An Analysis*, www.education.gov.uk/rsgateway/DB/STA/t000965/index.shtml

DfES (2003) *Every Child Matters*, London: The Stationery Office.

Douglas, D., Pavey, S., Clements, B. and Corcoran, C. (2009) *Network 1000. Visually impaired people's access to employment*, Visual Impairment Centre for Teaching and Research, School of Education, University of Birmingham for Vision2020.

Education and Skills Select Committee (2007) *Tenth Report. Special Educational Needs: Assessment and Funding*, HC 1077, 25 October.

Marschark, M. (2007) *Raising and Educating a Deaf Child*, Oxford: Oxford University Press.

Ofsted (2009) *Framework for the Inspection of Maintained Schools in England from September 2009*, Manchester: Ofsted.

Ofqual (2009) *Functional Skills Qualifications Criteria*, www.ofqual. gov.uk/qualification-and-assessment-framework/89-articles/238-functional-skills-criteria

Powers, S.G. (2009) 'Figuring out the Attainment', *BATOD Association Magazine*, May, pp 38–40.

Stobart, G. (2008) *Testing Times: The Uses and Abuses of Assessment*, Abingdon: Routledge.

Heading for inclusion: a head teacher's journey towards an inclusive school

Nigel Utton

Introduction

> While both humanization and dehumanization are real
> alternatives, only the first is man's vocation. This vocation is
> constantly negated, yet it is affirmed by that very negation.
> It is thwarted by injustice, exploitation, oppression, and the
> violence of the oppressors; it is affirmed by the yearning of
> the oppressed for freedom and justice, and by their struggle
> to recover their lost humanity. (Freire, 1972, p 20)

The Inclusion Movement is probably the most radical political
movement of our time. Not merely a group of educationalists talking
of including children in mainstream schooling (although we are that
too), we are a worldwide movement representing all the people of
the world calling for equality of resources, respect and opportunity.
The inclusive world we are building is very different from the *profit
before people* global economic system under which the majority of the
world currently lives. We are building a world in which, in the words
of Micheline Mason, 'each and every human being has a right to life,
to respect and to the means of participation in their societies' (Mason,
2000, p 118).

My personal journey to inclusion began long before I was born.
My genes contain the cultural memories handed down through
generations of Jewish and African enslavement, French Huguenot
protestant persecution, and white, working-class English oppression.
My family history, the tales we tell and our outlook on the world have
been shaped by historical forces larger than ourselves. My generation
has witnessed tremendous social, economic, political, technological
and cultural change. I was born only 20 years after the Second World

War where the projected fear of the few allowed for the attempted annihilation of the Jewish people, gypsies, homosexuals, communists and people with learning impairments. Who would have believed then that Nelson Mandela would become President of South Africa; that laws would protect the rights of women and gay people; that discrimination on the grounds of race and disability would be illegal; and that the United States of America would have a black president of African descent?

Given the social advances that we have made, why do children die every few seconds across the world from starvation while Europe has silos chock-full of perfectly useable food? Why are children with physical and intellectual impairments routinely taken away from their families and put in schools a long way from their home communities? And why are babies with an extra chromosome routinely aborted as though they are a worthless commodity?

> In our civilization we have modified our environment to such an extent during the cultural evolution that we have lost touch with our biological and ecological base more than any other culture and any other civilization in the past. This separation manifests itself in a striking disparity between the development of intellectual power, scientific knowledge, and technological skills on the one hand, and of wisdom, spirituality and ethics on the other. Scientific and technological knowledge has grown enormously since the Greeks embarked on the scientific venture in the sixth century B.C. But during these twenty-five centuries there has been hardly any progress in the conduct of social affairs. The spirituality and moral standards of Lao Tzu and Buddha, who also lived in the sixth century B.C. were clearly not inferior to ours. (Kapra, 1983, p 25)

Our collective political understanding and energy has not yet caught up with the technological advances that we have made, and the possibilities for creating a better world for all are being hampered by a global economic system that relies on stealing from the future to pay for the current greed and over-consumption of a small minority today.

I have worked as an inclusive primary school head teacher for five years. I was inspired into the profession by a sequence of dedicated teachers – good people – who chose to spend their lives educating young people by building their self-esteem and opening doors to their dreams. One primary school teacher, Tony Day, stands out for introducing himself as such to a surprised group of 10-year-olds in 1973, who were only used to calling teachers 'Mr' or 'Mrs'. Tony taught that the status quo can be challenged without society collapsing around our ears and that adults can treat young people with complete respect – valuing their thoughts and opinions.

It was while in Tony's class that our 'mainstream' school suffered a flood causing us to be temporarily moved to use the facilities of the children in the local 'special school'. This was one of those times of epoch-making importance in my personal development. Here we were, suddenly thrust among the cause of our greatest fear. The worst insults we could give to each other at school were homophobic taunts like 'poof' or the equally offensive 'Brooky', Brookfields being the name of the local school for 'weirdoes, freaks, loonies' – subhuman people whom we were supposed never to meet. How would we cope with being amongst these children – the stuff of nightmares! To our amazement, after some initial teasing (effectively handled by Tony), we became friends with many of the children and felt quite upset when we were taken back to our repaired school after a couple of weeks. My world view was irrevocably changed. I could not comprehend why those children were separated from the rest of us – it made no sense whatsoever. For me this was absolute proof that adults do not get things right, that we, the children, could actually make better decisions than them. That is a very frightening thought for a child to have, rather like the boy in Hans Christian Andersen's story who realises that the Emperor actually has no clothes. I have spent much of my professional life getting into a position where that opinion can finally be heard!

I joined the British Red Cross when I was about seven, learning to do first aid and enjoying the company of other young people. It was through the Red Cross that I first became actively involved in work with young people with physical and intellectual impairments. For several years running, I worked as a care assistant on holidays 'looking after' other young boys like myself who just happened to have something 'wrong' with their body. I knew nothing at the time of the social model of disability and I am sure my initial motivation was from a position of Christian 'charitable' giving, which I now see to be patronising, disempowering and more for boosting my own feeling of self-worth. Despite that confusion, the opportunity did give me a very useful insight into the way people with impairments are *mis*treated and educated me into seeing more effective ways of empowering them. Life-changing moments for me were: first, watching a football match in which 'carers' were playing a fast and furious game *around* children with impairments making no allowance for their physical needs –

resulting in one young boy with a life-threatening heart complaint having the ball kicked hard into his chest, which could have killed him; and, second, convincing a more experienced 'carer' to allow us to take wheelchair-using children to the top of a high flight of steps rather than leave them at the bottom while the rest of us went to look at a spectacular view. Being inclusive does not mean all children must do exactly the same thing – it means that we intelligently challenge our expectation of what can be achieved.

During the football match, I remember feeling a sense of profound powerlessness as the adults leading the activity would not listen to my warnings. They continued to power the ball around the field amongst the children – showing off their physical prowess. Even after the young boy was hit they continued to play the game and I remember leaving the field devastated, crying and begging a friend to intervene to stop the game. Looking back, that was a pivotal moment in realising that I need never again act powerless around injustice.

Spending six months as a student in the Soviet Union in 1984/85 was a revelation. The faults of that system are well documented. The successes of the Russian Revolution, however, receive far less attention. I saw a people working together for the good of all, truly sharing resources and giving generously of their humanity in a way I had not experienced living in the West. I was struck by the collective pride and desire for all to contribute and receive from society. (I returned to a Britain where Margaret Thatcher reportedly said there is *no* society.) As an English student, I was asked to join a group of young people who went to Yevgeny Yevtushenko's house each day to do 'patterning' with his son, Tosha, who had learning impairments. I know some of my friends in the Inclusion Movement have some questions about patterning, but I found the process a very positive one and was able to see definite benefits to Tosha, whose speech and movement improved over the period I was there.

I was fascinated by the differences in the ways the students supported Tosha. We fell into two camps: one group would get Tosha through the exercises as quickly as possible and help him to pass over, or even ignore, the ones he did not like; the other group, of which I was a part, trusted the process and insisted that Tosha really challenge himself to go through each exercise the way it was designed – sometimes causing tears. The latter course had the more profound effect, allowing Tosha to really develop and theoretically retrain his neurones to take better control of his speech, movement and thought. I now know that the tears that Tosha shed were an essential part of the process – enabling him to 'discharge' the accumulated distress and allow new neurone pathways to grow in his brain. I still see these two differing approaches in the education system where some teachers go through the motions year after year with children with learning impairments, never really challenging them to deepen their learning – never having high expectations of their achievement.

Learning to be an inclusive teacher

On finishing my languages degree I wanted to spend time with my two-year-old daughter so took a part-time job as Norwich Toy Librarian. The Hamlet Centre had been set up by Margaret and Jack Wymer, two wheelchair users who had passed through the segregated school system just after the war. Margaret and Jack were inspirational. They told a sanitised version of their release from segregated living in their book *Another Door Opens* (Wymer and Wymer, 1980). They were afraid to tell the true story because many of the 'carers' were still alive and they generously did not want to malign the individuals. Their nobility of spirit is akin to Nelson Mandela's approach towards a system that confined him to prison for 27 years. My education at Margaret and Jack's side profoundly affected my approach to children. Seeing Margaret listen with complete respect to young people who had been condemned to the scrap heap of low expectations was truly moving. I see the same profound understanding when Micheline Mason (inclusion activist and author) listens patiently to young people with learning difficulties or communication impairments. On a good day as head teacher I am able to give my time to individual young people and am able to draw on the wonderful examples that I have been set in my own education:

> Learners need to feel that they are doing well. They always are, but this requires basic philosophical clarification for many teachers to understand. The point is that the learners are always doing the very best they can if one takes into account (which is the only realistic thing to do) all the tensions and pressures which drag upon them. If they are all doing the very best that they can do, then they are doing very well. If the teacher sincerely communicates to them that they are doing very well, this in itself relaxes the grip of the tensions upon them and automatically leads to their doing better. (Jackins, 1991, p 119)

As a young person I had attended state primary and comprehensive schools. I had every intention *not* to be a school teacher. (Although looking back I was clearly fighting against my destiny – rather like the Jewish joke: 'What makes God laugh most?' 'When people start their prayers ... "I have got this plan ...".') Growing up in Thatcher's Britain, I had seen the disdain poured upon teachers and how they were blamed for just society's ills. When Sir Keith Joseph, the then Secretary of State for Education, came to my secondary school I was asked, as Head Boy, to do a welcoming speech. I remember the huge applause from the sixth-formers and teachers when I gave a passionate speech condemning his plans to give grants for young people to go to private schools and said he should be supporting the comprehensive system instead. I remember feeling what a tragic situation that a senior politician could not see the social damage his policies were doing – while I, a mere teenager, could.

When looking for a nursery for my daughter I discovered Norwich Montessori School, which instantly took my attention. Unlike the other nurseries where I saw adults going through the motions – even to the extent of tidying up the faces on cotton wool snowmen so they would all look the same – here I saw truly personalised learning. All children working at their own pace, all engaged in different activities and being 'observed' by the staff at a distance so as not to interfere with the learning process. The school was inclusive of a small group of European Muslim children, black African, white Protestant and Catholic English children and one child, Dylan, with profound learning difficulties. Here I first saw inclusion in action. It did not matter that Dylan could not speak or that the cultural and religious differences of the children were profound. Each child was a part of the whole, while their own unique contribution was respected and celebrated.

As a teenager I discovered the writings of A.S. Neill (1966) and his wonderful Summerhill School. Started around the same time as the Russian Revolution, Summerhill was born out of an exciting and energetic time where radical politics and education came together in a flourishing of new thought and experiment across the world. While our present-day politicians tinker with the idea of student councils and pupil participation, Summerhill has been living that as a core ethos for nearly a hundred years. Summerhill does not merely pay lip service to pupils having a voice on trivial immaterial decision-making or give half-hour lessons on *citizenship*. The pupils of Summerhill get a real sense of their power as individuals and collectively in the actual running of their school. The Friday meeting I attended at Summerhill had as its main agenda item whether or not the school should have a half-term holiday – the school chose not to! As we move closer to inclusive education we must allow our children to take much greater charge of their learning institutions – and to really experience democratic decision-making concerning their own futures:

> Education is a people enterprise and relationships are the key to the successful accomplishment of its primary resource. There is no school improvement or curriculum development without people development. The quality of interpersonal relationships – between staff and between staff and pupils – is the greatest single factor in the development of the school as a learning community and therefore of gains for all its students. It is the relationship between teacher and learner, not the technical skills of teaching, which are the strongest determinant of what a child learns. (Mahony, 2004)

I started my teaching career in inner-city Portsmouth. The children were vibrant, energetic and a joy to be among. Many of the children had 'learning difficulties' and nearly all came from economically deprived homes. Their achievement on tests was low and their reading ages were usually far below their chronological ages. Their social interactions were chaotic and impulsive. The received wisdom was that the children were 'kinaesthetic learners' who needed practical-based work with little academic stretch. It was clear to me that these children were bright and potentially academically sparkling! Once again I was encountering settling for less than is possible. To prove the point, I asked to teach a group of underachieving readers. In only six hour-long sessions I moved their reading ages forward an average of 18 months. Not by teaching a boring, pedestrian, technical, phonic-based curriculum – but by reading and performing dynamic, energetic poetry, playing with the words, pushing the children beyond where they thought they could go, *expecting* them to learn to read. I took a similar approach to dyslexic children who were scared to make mistakes in their writing because they had been mocked either by others or by themselves for doing so in the past. I encouraged them to deliberately get it wrong! To get 0/10 in their spelling test; to write a whole page of work that I could not read – sending them away to do it again if there was a word spelled correctly! Playing with the children – laughing, building a close personal relationship – and allowing them to talk and cry when they found it hard.

My teaching career coincided with my introduction to Re-evaluation Co-counselling (RC). The theory of RC fitted well with the model of the world that I had developed through my past experiences. I joined Portsmouth RC men's group and for the first time in my life experienced 'listening'. Being listened to by a human with no hidden agenda, no set formula and no expectation or judgement was a profound experience. Over the years, RC has developed a theory and practice that continually examines our place in society and gives us a way of liberating ourselves both from the effects of past experiences of distress as individuals and from the oppression experienced by the different groups to which we belong. Through being listened to effectively by our peers we are able to 'discharge' (talk, laugh, cry, yawn, shake) the effects of old hurts and gain a clearer understanding of our motivations and behavioural patterns. The one-point programme of RC is to 'recover a person's full intelligence and to help others to do the same'.

I took this understanding into my role as Teacher in Charge of an EBD unit (for children with 'emotional and behavioural difficulties'). The 'unit' was initially a room within a mainstream primary school in one of the largest council estates in Europe. It is an area of high deprivation with attendant social and economic issues. When I started, the 'unit' was populated by boys and one girl with a range of labels who interacted rarely with their mainstream peers. They were subject to a different behavioural regime and even had different start and finish times. All of them came from beyond the normal catchment area for the school.

The received wisdom regarding children with behavioural difficulties was (and largely still is) based soundly in behaviourist theory. Children are bad and need to be rewarded to become good. This does not fit with my personal experience or the view of the world as explained in RC theory (for a deeper discussion, see Kapra, 1983). Children are born *good*. Children look out into a world for love and closeness with other human beings and usually do not find sufficient of it to allow them to keep a sense of their own full worth. On the contrary, they are often greeted with long periods of isolation, neglect and sometimes even hostility, abuse and violence.

Different groups within society are oppressed for the colour of their skin, their religious observance, the economic well-being of their parents, their gender – basically any way in which they are different from the perceived dominant group. By the age of four, when children start school, they have already absorbed their carers' behavioural patterns and already have an unconscious understanding of their permitted place within society – already having experienced the oppression meted out on their particular group of humans: black boys who enter school 'with a chip on their shoulders' (and yes I have heard teachers say that) do so because they have already been subject to racism from the moment they were born; Jewish children already carry the terror and mistrust passed on through generations of persecution – and so on with each group targeted for special oppression.

It is not unusual for children to start school exhibiting violent language and behaviour. A reward chart targeting the end of anti-social behaviours simply trains the child to *mask the symptoms* of their particular oppression. These days the reward chart is often backed up with drugs, prescribed arbitrarily, to quieten the child down and force them to fit into the system, which, I would argue, is part of the cause of their malaise. These children do not need reward and punishment, and they certainly *do not need drugs* – they need a damned good listening to!

To compound the devastating effect of oppression, as a result of the capitalisation of food production and the deliberate targeting of children by advertising for processed foodstuffs, the 21st-century child's diet is highly inadequate in essential nutrients resulting in food intolerances, nutritional deficiencies and erratic behaviours. Many young people come into school in the morning having only eaten a packet of crisps and a can of highly sweetened carbonated drink.

I took on the job in the 'unit' knowing that the head teacher was keen to bring the children into the heart of the mainstream school. My first job was to support the staff and pupils in doing that. RC taught me the need to think flexibly in every situation and not to rely on past responses:

> The reliable criterion for distinguishing rational from reactive behaviour turns out to be the question of its rigidity or flexibility. The response is rational if it is new, accurate and workable in the particular situation. It is recorded and irrational if it is old, repetitive and ineffective. One cannot determine the rationality of a particular attitude or response by whether the person making it reports feeling 'good' or 'bad'. (Jackins, 1991, p 74)

Re-educating children out of a behaviourist model was not easy. They had been used to special treatment and resented having to lose their 'privileges' over the rest of the school. All of the children were of a similar academic standard to their peers and I could see no reason why, without emotional support, they could not be fully included in the life of the rest of the school. I changed the system of punishment/reward (given on a Friday afternoon depending upon the number of points the children had received during the week) for a system of guaranteed 'circle of friends' time in which the child and a group of their peers, who volunteered to be part of the group, came together to play games, get to know each other and to discuss the events both good and bad that had happened during the week. These were usually very enjoyable sessions, often very powerful and always resulting in deepening the relationships between the young people themselves and with me. I taught the children RC theory and explained about 'discharge' as a way of releasing pent-up emotion. The children were encouraged to talk, laugh, cry, shake and yawn to help release their emotions. They became effective listeners for each other and became very bold about challenging behavioural patterns that had a negative effect. Throughout this time, I had regular counselling sessions myself to ensure my decisions were as clear as possible and to stretch me to keep my thinking flexible. This version of the circle of friends had no hierarchy and an observer would not know which were the 'normal' children and which were the 'EBD' children. There were times when all of the children would have needs with which the group was able to provide support. Visitors to our 'unit' were always surprised that the room was usually empty and the children were in 'normal' mainstream classrooms. It was at this point – about two years in – that we changed the name to 'provision' for children with emotional and behavioural difficulties.

The educational establishment seems to have a need to label and give names to behaviours and to systems or approaches. I therefore called my system 'normality therapy'. The children in the 'unit' were given a 'normal' experience of school. They were treated like the rest of the school, expected to follow the same behaviour policy and play a full and active part in the life of the school. They were included in a particular class, included on the register, given the same opportunities as the rest of the children. Year after year one class elected a boy with a statement for 'EBD' to be their representative on the school council because they knew he would stand up and be counted on their behalf and not be afraid to put a point of view! Another of the boys took a lead part in the school play. Normal opportunities, which are every child's birthright.

Drawing on my experience with the Red Cross, I was able to ensure that the children were not simply thrown into the deep end of the classroom experience and expected to swim. Assistants worked closely with the children to support them and enable them to get the best out of the learning environment. The teachers were very skilled in differentiating activities to give the children the best possible learning opportunities and possibilities for success. We did provide a space for the children to come when things became too hard for them in class – and this was used by 'mainstream' children too!

Failures in the name of inclusion

> "Segregation now! Segregation tomorrow! Segregation for ever!" That was in January 1963 when he [George Wallace] stood 'in the schoolhouse door' of the University of Alabama and prevented the enrolment of the first black students under the Kennedy administration's desegregation laws. (Pilger, 1989, p 132)

It took unparalleled bravery and the risk of death to stand up to the horrors of Nazi ideology and the bigotry of racism in the United States and South Africa. The current renaissance of fascism in Europe and extreme Muslim and Christian fundamentalism across the world is testament to a global world view that has not yet unburdened itself from a history of intolerance and hatred. By embracing inclusion and therefore tackling all forms of prejudice, schools are addressing that issue with the next generation and starting the world on a long-term road of greater justice and equality of opportunity.

Extremist groups project their fear onto people different from themselves. Black people, Jews, Muslims, indigenous peoples, Protestants, Catholics, homosexuals, women and people with physical and intellectual impairments are all targeted by society for destruction. Not to embrace inclusion is to succumb to a tyranny of fear; fear of the 'Other'; fear of daring to live with difference. We all suffer from such a world view:

> In writing this book and allowing us to share in their experiences, Jack and Margaret Wymer give us all the chance to see that risk, choice and independence are essential elements in the growth of their relationship and their life together. Apart from the significance of this to themselves they have taught the able-bodied something about living. Their greatest achievement, however, is in demonstrating that the apparently impossible can be done, thereby making it harder for society to deny the same opportunity for independence to other people with handicaps. (George Meredith, Director of Social Services, Norfolk County Council, in Wymer and Wymer, 1980, Preface)

There is not a coherent understanding of the term inclusion. Special schools often claim to be 'doing inclusion' when they give outreach to mainstream schools – or when they allow one labelled group to mix temporarily with another. This view of inclusion is based in the medical model of disability that classifies students in a 19th-century pseudo-scientific manner. Needs are defined and organised with children being sorted into groups and filed into schools under the relevant category. The special needs industry in England depends upon this perverse system, allowing fortunes to be made by private educational establishments, 'experts' and mostly by the legal profession. Speaking recently to a governor of a well-known and well-respected charitable school for deaf children, I was appalled at the depth of his segregationist mentality, which enabled him to actually laugh at the fact that the hearing-impaired young people have to 'sneak out' to find companionship with hearing children and, worse still, are forbidden from using British Sign Language. In an inclusive school all children would learn BSL!

The special needs industry cynically promotes segregated education in the guise of protecting poor little children with special needs from the horrors of mainstream schooling. Rather like the 19th-century charitable institutions described in *Incurably Human* (Mason, 2000), they clean up society by keeping the 'deserving poor' out of the public eye. We can all appease our consciences by giving generously. Local authorities collectively spend millions of pounds each year either ferrying children with impairments around in taxis to segregated schools or paying enormous private education bills. Even worse, they spend millions in paying solicitors, barristers and 'experts' to appear in SEN Tribunals to decide the fate of children with additional needs.

As it stands, even the state school system works against inclusion. With its unnatural obsession with measurement, accountability and 'standards', the curriculum is skewed to fit the child into a model that will be judged by simplistic, fickle and ill-thought-out Ofsted criteria. It is seen as desirable for certain schools *not* to accept children with learning or physical impairments and certainly children with challenging behaviour. There are easy ways for schools to make it difficult for parents to bring their children with special needs. All head teachers know of colleagues who make it clear to parents that their child's needs would be so much better catered for in the school down the road. I even know of one '*outstanding*' head teacher who puts post-it notes on her wall when she visits the local nurseries reminding her which children not to admit! Parents of children with Down's syndrome and other visible impairments talk movingly of their experiences trying to find a welcoming school for their child. Ofsted would do well to talk to the parents of children with special needs who are in the catchment area of, but who do not attend, 'outstanding' schools. Ofsted does not comment on why a particular school seems to have fewer children with special needs than its neighbours! There is a piece of work to be done comparing the Ofsted grades for schools with high levels of deprivation and special needs with those that do not!

I was recently shocked, although not surprised, during inclusion training, which I was presenting for Church schools, to hear an 'outstanding' head teacher blurt out:"I have seen the devastation that a child with Down's syndrome can cause to a school."What experience must that poor child have had – and what messages were unconsciously conveyed to the rest of the children?

Those of us with inclusive schools have seen the delight and joy that children with Down's syndrome can bring to a school community. In my current school, I cannot explain the thrill I felt the first time that 'L', who has Down's syndrome, actually replied to my 'good morning' – having said 'good morning' to her probably 50 mornings before – or the pride on seeing how our children with sensory impairments are guided gently and thoughtfully around our school by their friends. For inclusion to become widespread, it will be necessary for a change of educational philosophy that values the development of people as members of society above neat and tidy, simplistic measures of attainment.

Inclusion at work

St Georges School in Harpenden is one of the few secondary schools in this country where boys and girls are educated together. On last Speech Day several favourable opinions were expressed on the subject of co-education. In his annual report the Head Master pleaded for more helpers in the cause of this form of education, which, he said, helped the life of boys and girls at that point where help was most needed.

The Bishop of London, who gave away the prizes, said that he had come there with a mind completely open on the subject of co-education, to see the first school of boys and girls brought up together which had come under his notice and he was favourably impressed. If they could change the tone of society on the moral question to the healthy tone

existing in the school, they could certainly accomplish one
of the finest things in the world, concluded the Bishop.
(Roger Ascham, *The Schoolmaster*, 1909, reproduced in
NUT, 2009)

Despite being the most wonderful, rewarding and exciting project,
inclusive education is hard. State schools are funded on an optimum class
size of 30. This is not an ideal environment for the inclusion of *any* child!
State schools, however, do a magnificent job in making the misdirected,
underfunded system work for children. What is often forgotten is that
within the class of 30, with perhaps one full-time teacher and some
teaching assistant time, there are also 30 other intelligences at work.
Children can and, with encouragement from the teacher, usually do
support each other extremely well. I would not want the 'powers that
be' to take this as an excuse for continuing oversized classes – but,
equally, while we are in the transition from segregated to inclusive
education, head teachers must use all the resources at their disposal to
ensure the best possible education for all children. Our school system
is dependent on good relationships. We, thankfully, no longer physically
beat children into submission (although some schools are still run with
a climate of fear). Circles of support are a powerful way of building
closer relationships between young people and with adults, and I have
seen various models depending on the needs of specific children. The
trick is always to:

1. ask the child at the centre what they need;
2. use our own thinking to see whether that is possible or desirable; and
3. in consultation with the children in the group, put a plan into action.

I have seen such a system work for so many children: one major success
was a boy whose mother would regularly try to commit suicide. (The
medical model said the boy had emotional problems and required
medication.) He would come into school, find a place to hide and curl
himself up into a ball. (A perfectly normal reaction to the situation, in
my opinion.) His circle of friends was a constant reminder that he was
liked and supported and played a huge role in enabling him to have a
'normal' time at school. Had he been in a school purely for children
with similar emotional trauma, he would never have experienced this
'normality therapy'.

Another benefit of circles of support is to the rest of the children. *All*
children have periods in their life where things are not going so well
and they need support from others. Being part of a circle of friends

allows any participant to bring forward difficulties that they want to share with the group. During my four years as Teacher in Charge, children brought forward: bereavement, divorce, sibling violence, racism, bullying, sexism and homophobic bullying, to name but a few issues. The inclusion of children with presenting emotional difficulties forces a school to address these issues for all children. Just as the Disability Discrimination Act improves access for all people, so inclusion improves education for all children. Schools that do not embrace this concept may well be better placed to have selective cohorts of high-achieving children, but they are not fulfilling their essential role of creating people for a 21st-century inclusive world.

When I look out at my school during assembly and see different skin colours, different religions, children with physical, sensory and intellectual impairments, and boys and girls who are living and playing together – not always getting it right, but working so hard to get along with one another and learn together – I have a vision of a world where we are not terrified of difference and where we accept and celebrate those around us. Inclusion is the only educational system that will help us to build that world. We have shown the way. We now need our politicians to have the moral courage to actively promote and support schools to do the right thing – now!

References

Freire, P. (1972) *Pedagogy of the Oppressed*, London: Pelican.

Jackins, H. (1991) *The Human Situation*, Seattle: Rational Island Publishers.

Kapra, F. (1983) *The Turning Point*, London: Flamingo Paperbacks.

Mahony, T. (2004) *Principled Headship*, Carmarthen: Crown House Publishing Ltd.

Neill, A.S. (1966) *Summerhill*, London: Victor Gollancz Ltd.

NUT (2009) *The Teacher Magazine*, July, London.

Pilger, J. (1989) *Heroes*, London: Pan Books.

Wymer, J. and Wymer, M. (1980) *Another Door Opens*, London: Souvenir Press.

Suggested further reading

Allen, J. (1999) *Actively Seeking Inclusion: Pupils with Special Needs in Mainstream Schools*, London: Falmer Press.

Armstrong, F. (2003) *Spaced Out: Policy, Difference and the Challenge of Inclusive Education*, London: Kluwer.

Armstrong, F. and Barton, L. (eds) (1999) *Disability, Human Rights and Education*, Buckingham: Open University Press.

Armstrong, F. and Richards, G. (eds) (2007) *Including Teaching Assistants: Developing Understanding and Practice in Inclusive Education*, London: Routledge.

Ballard, K. (ed) (1999) *Inclusive Education: International Voices on Disability and Justice*, London: Falmer.

Barnes, C. (1981) *Disabled People in Britain and Discrimination: A Case for Anti-Discrimination Legislation*, London: Hurst.

Barnes, C. and Mercer, G. (2004) *Disability, Policy and Practice: Applying the Social Model*, Leeds: The Disability Press.

Barnes, C., Oliver, M. and Barton, L. (eds) (2002) *Disability Studies Today*, Oxford: Polity Press.

Barton, L. (ed) (1996) *Disability and Society: Emerging Issues and Insights*, Harlow: Pearson Education Ltd.

Barton, L. (ed) (2001) *Disability, Politics and the Struggle for Change*, London: David Fulton Publishers.

Barton, L. (ed) (2007) *Education and Society: 25 years of the British Journal of Education*, London: Routledge.

Barton, L. and Armstrong, F. (eds) (2007) *Policy, Experience and Change: Cross-Cultural Reflections on Inclusive Education*, London: Springer.

Booth, T. and Ainscow, M. (1998) *From Them to Us: An International Study of Inclusion in Education*, London: Routledge.

Borsay, A. (2005) *Disability and Social Policy in Britain since 1750: A History of Exclusion*, Basingstoke: Palgrave Macmillan.

British Journal of Sociology of Education (2010) vol 31, no 5, Special Issue 'The Sociology of Disability and Education'.

Corker, M. and Davis, J. (2002) 'Portrait of Callum. The Disabling of a Childhood?' in R. Edwards (ed) *Children, Home and School: Regulation, Autonomy or Connection?*, London: Routledge Falmer.

Davis, J., Watson, N., Corker, M. and Shakespeare, T. (2003) 'Reconstructing Disability, Childhood and Social Policy in the UK', in C. Hallett and A. Prout (eds) *Hearing the Voices of Children: Social Policy for a New Century*, London: Routledge Falmer.

Florian, L. and McLaughlin, M.J. (2008) *Disability Classification in Education: Issues and Perspectives*, Thousand Oaks, CA: Corwin Press.

French, S. (2006) *An Oral History of the Education of Visually Impaired People*, Lewiston, Queenston and Lampeter: Edwin Mellen Press.

Fulcher, G. (1999) *Disabling Policies? A Comparative Approach to Education and Disability*, Sheffield: Philip Armstrong Publications.

Fuller, M., Georgeson, J., Healey, M., Hurst, A., Kelly, K., Riddell, S., Roberts, H. and Weedon, E. (2009) *Improving Disabled Students' Learning: Experiences and Outcomes,* London: Routledge.

Haines, S. (2006) *14–19 Education and Training and Young Disabled People: A Working Draft of Ideas*, Nuffield Review of 14–19 Education and Training, Working Paper 37.

Humphries, S. and Gordon, P. (1992) *Out of Sight: The Experience of Disability 1900–1950*, Plymouth: Northcote House.

Hurt, J. S. (1988) *Outside the Mainstream: A History of Special Education*, London: Batsford.

Jackson, L. (2002) *Freaks, Geeks and Asperger Syndrome: A User Guide to Adolescence*, London: Jessica Kingsley Publishers.

Kluth, P. (2003) *You're Going to Love This Kid! Teaching Students with Autism in the Inclusive Classroom*, Baltimore, Paul H Brookes Publishing Co., Inc.

Komulainen, S. (2007) 'The Ambiguity of the Child's "Voice" in Social Research', in *Childhood*, vol 14, no 1, pp 11–28.

Kristiansen, K., Vehmas, S. and Shakespeare, T. (eds) (2008) *Arguing about Disability: Philosophical Perspectives*, London: Routledge.

Lewis, A., Parsons, S. and Robertson, C. (2007) *My School, My Family, My Life: Telling It Like It Is. A Study Drawing on the Experiences of Disabled Children, Young People and Their Families in Great Britain in 2006*, London/Birmingham: Disability Rights Commission/University of Birmingham, School of Education.

Mahony, T. (1999) *Principled Headship: A Teacher's Guide to the Galaxy*, Carmarthen: Crown House Publishing.

Mason, M. (2000) *Incurably Human*, London: Working Press.

Morris, J. (2002) *A Lot to Say. A Guide for Social Workers, Personal Advisors and Others Working with Disabled Children and Young People with Communication Impairments*, London: Scope.

Neill, A. S. (1953) *The Free Child*, London: Herbert Jenkins Ltd.

Neill, A. S. (1966) *Summerhill: A Radical Approach to Education*, London: Victor Gollancz Ltd.

Nind, M. (2009) *Conducting Qualitative Research with People with Learning, Communication and Other Disabilities: Methodological Challenges*, National Centre for Research Methods, ESRC National Centre for Research Methods Review Paper, NCRM/012. Available at: http://eprints.soton.ac.uk/65065/

Nind, M., Sheehy, K. and Simmons, K. (eds) (2003) *Inclusive Education: Learners and Learning Contexts*, London: David Fulton.

Oliver, M. and Campbell, J. (1996) *Disability Politics*, London: Routledge.

Prime Minister's Strategy Unit (2005) *Improving the Life Chances of Disabled People*, London: Prime Minister's Strategy Unit/Cabinet Office.

Read, J., Clements, L. and Ruebain, D. (2006) *Disabled Children and the Law: Research and Good Practice*, 2nd edn, London: Jessica Kingsley.

Riddell, S. (2006) *Policy and Practice in Special Educational Needs*, 2nd edn, Edinburgh: Dunedin Academic Press.

Riddell, S., Tinklin, T. and Wilson, A. (2005) *Disabled Students in Higher Education*, London: Routledge Falmer.

Shakespeare, T. (2006) *Disability Rights and Wrongs*, London: Routledge.

Skrtic, T. M. (ed) (1995) *Disability and Democracy*, London: Teachers College Press.

Sutherland, G. (1984) *Ability, Merit and Measurement: Mental Testing and English Education, 1880–1940*, Oxford: Clarendon Press.

Terzi, L. (2005) 'Beyond the Dilemma of Difference: The Capability Approach on Disability and Special Educational Needs', *Journal of Philosophy of Education*, 39(3), pp 443–59.

Todd, L. (2007) *Partnerships for Inclusive Education: A Critical Approach to Collaborative Working,* London: Routledge.

Tomlinson, S. (1982) *A Sociology of Special Education*, London: Routledge and Kegan Paul.

Warnock, M. (1978) *Report of the Committee of Enquiry into the Education of Handicapped Children and Young People* (the Warnock Report), London: HMSO.

Watson, N., Shakespeare, T., Cunningham-Burley, S., Barnes, C., Corker, M., Davis, J. and Priestly, M. (1999) *Life as a Disabled Child: A Qualitative Study of Young People's Experiences and Perspectives*, ESRC Research Programme 'Children 5–16: Growing into the Twenty-First Century', Grant number L129251047.

Williams, D. (1994) *Somebody Somewhere: Breaking Free from the World of Autism*, London: Jessica Kingsley Publishers.

Index

D

Danforth, S. 77
Darwin, Charles 8
Day, Tony 162-3
deaf children
education methods in historical
context 12
see also children with sensory
impairment
deficit model *see* individual deficit
model of disability
degeneration discourse 8
Department for Children, Schools
and Families (DCSF) 39, 91, 105
and assessment of children with
sensory impairment 155
Children's Plan 108, 122-3, 123-4
'Think Family' agenda 106, 121
direct payments and individual
budgets 33-4, 37, 60, 112, 119,
120, 124
Disability Debate 51
Disability Discrimination Act (1995)
2, 4, 18, 29, 33, 35, 123
and categorisation of disabilities 133
entry into professions and 'fitness to
practice' standards 140, 144
qualifications and examination 158
and scope of SEN framework 51-3,
148
Disability Discrimination Act (2005)
114
disability discrimination law
lack of rights-based approach in
education 51-3
positive and negative rights 26, 29,
40
rights-based approach to SEN 59-
60
and Statement of SEN 29-30
see also Disability Discrimination Act
Disability Equality Duty (DED) 29-
30, 51-2, 59, 106, 114
disability equality schemes in
universities 133
Disability Rights Commission 53,
116-17, 123, 140, 145*n*
disabled children *see* children with
disabilities
Disabled Persons (Services,
Consultation and Representation)
Act (1986) 31

Disabled Students' Allowance (DSA)
132-3, 134, 141
disadvantage and disabled children
69-70, 93-4, 100, 110-11, 125
and access to higher education 134,
135, 137, 143-4
and early intervention approach
107-9
disclosure dilemma for disabled
students 141-3
disempowerment
attitudes towards impairment 163-4
families
'passive helper' role of parents 77,
78-9
and 'statementing' process 14-15
historical context 8
Down, John Langdon 12
Dunst, C. 111
dyslexia 97, 167
in university students 132, 134, 135,
138-9, 141-3

E

early intervention approach 106, 107-
9, 113
Early Intervention Fund 106
Early Support Programme: Family
Service Plan 118-19
EBD (emotional and behavioural
difficulties) unit 168-71
Economic and Social Research
Council: Teaching and Learning
Research Programme 132
education
attainment levels for disabled
children 16, 111
children with sensory impairment
152-5
lack of expectations 16, 51, 167
need for improvement in whole-
system context 47, 52-3, 69, 72
and partnership 122-3
personalised approach 112-13, 124,
166
policy interaction with law on social
care 25-6, 30-6
parallel conflicting approaches
25-6, 40-1
right to education 18, 47
'capabilities approach' 58-62
human rights-based approach 54-5

O

offenders with learning disabilities 51
Ofqual 153, 156-7, 158-9
Ofsted 38, 157, 172-3
  inclusiveness evaluation 71
  *Special Educational Needs and
    Disability Review* 47, 52
  Tellus survey 91, 97
opportunity *see* equality of
    opportunity
oppression and effect on children
    168-9

P

parent advisers in schools 122-3
Parent Councils 122
Parent Forums 121, 123
Parent Partnership Services 114, 123
'parent power' 123
parent–professional partnerships 69,
    78, 108, 111-14, 119, 120-1, 122-3
parental choice and SEN framework
    23-4, 24-5, 40-1, 72
  and equality of opportunity 49
  and human rights focus on interests
    of child 55
  and legal approaches to education
    and care law 36, 37-9, 40-1, 59-60
  policy and decrease in 50-1
  and 'statementing' process
    appeals procedure 27-8
    lack of determination 14
  see also families
parental consent and voice of child 93
parental perspectives and multi-
    agency working 75-81
participation
  children and parents 77-8, 90, 118,
    125
    Parent Forums 121, 123
  children in schools 166-7
  see also consultation with children
    and parents; higher education
    participation; partnership;
    segregation; voice of the child
Partlett, M. 77
partnership
  and education 122-3
  parents and professionals 69, 78, 108,
    111-14, 119, 120-1, 122-3

'people, practice, context' model
    80-1
  see also multi-agency working
'passive helper' role of parents 77,
    78-9
'patterning' 164-5
'people, practice, context' (PPC)
    partnership model 80
'person-centred learning' 56, 57
'person-centred' service delivery 57
personal tutors in schools 122
personalisation
  and education 112-13, 124, 166
  and social care 33-6, 60, 106, 112,
    119, 120, 124
Pilger, J. 171
Plowden Report (1967) 67
politics and bias towards inclusion 3,
    23, 48, 51
population change and policy 109-11
poverty *see* disadvantage and disabled
    children
Powers, S.G. 151-2
pressure groups 72, 79
PricewaterhouseCoopers 120-1
Prime Minister's Strategy Unit 105,
    107, 113
Prison Reform Trust 51
prisoners with learning disabilities 51
'privilege cognisant' professionals 66,
    80-1
professions and disability
  and construction of identities and
    roles 77-9
  disclosure of disability and 'fitness to
    practice' 139-43, 144
  historical context 12-15, 70
  parent–professional partnerships 69,
    78, 108, 111-14, 119, 120-1, 122-3
  see also multi-agency working
Prouty, Robert 61-2
psychology profession and special
    education 13-14, 70, 79
Public Service Agreement Indicator
    54 121
public services
  spending cuts 3, 5
  and higher education fees 133-4
  see also Disability Equality Duty;
    local authorities; service delivery
Pupil and Parent Guarantees 113